YOUR SOUL'S TARGET

How to aim for your destiny in the midst of distractions

STYLAND SCOTT

YOUR *SOUL'S* TARGET

How to aim for your destiny in the midst of distractions

STYLAND SCOTT

A Small Independant Publisher
With A Big Voice

Printed in the United States of America by
T&J Publishers (Atlanta, GA.)
www.TandJPublishers.com

All Bible verses used are from the King James Bible and the New International Version (NIV) Bible.

Cover design by Timothy Flemming, Jr. (T&J Publishers)
Book format and layout by Timothy Flemming, Jr. (T&J Publishers)

ISBN: 978-0-9981621-0-2

To contact author, go to:
yoursoulstarget.wixsite.com/ontarget
yoursoulstarget@gmail.com
Facebook: Bishop Styland Scott

ACKNOWLEDGMENTS

I am so grateful to so many God has given me to love, care, and show compassion.

I want to thank my wife, my son, my mother and father, my family, my friends, my church supporters, and the body of Christ for allowing me to take the time to receive from God what He would have us to know and to line up our lives for an eternal life with him.

A special thank you to Pastor Timothy Fleming, Jr. for your assistance, skills and abilities to make this possible. I never thought I would be used to write a book, even with the gift of writing music and gospel plays for so many years. God alone inspired me to write this book and I pray it will be a blessing to those who truly read each line and take a personal assessment as to the decision they have made to target Heaven as their eternal home. The Bible says God desires for "all to be saved and come into the Glory of God." It is your passion that drives me and your support that moves me.

TABLE OF CONTENTS

FOREWORD

I HAVE ALWAYS WONDERED AS A YOUNG GIRL GROWING UP why the "things of God" were always so heavy in my spirit and on my mind. This book has helped me to realize that my soul was longing to be steered in the direction of heaven. No wonder I was always intrigued with the organization named Upward Bound. Growing up in a small baptist church where the doctrine of heaven and hell was constantly preached every Sunday, I felt as if I needed to make a choice and target my life to successfully reach the most important goal in life: heaven. Life brought many major distractions and temptations in my younger years, causing me to often get off target and miss the mark. Romans 3:23 says, "For everyone has sinned; we all fall short of God's glorious standard" (NIV).

I am so thankful to God for keeping me in His care and leading me through life's ups and downs. Thank you Bishop Styland Scott for writing this God-inspired book to help us to continue to focus, press, aim, and reach our desired target: Heaven. You have clearly instructed us on redirecting our spiritual eyesight away from distractions and the "things that so easily beset us."

I pray the Lord use this book to open our hearts and minds to constantly take notice of our lives and check the order of our arrows so that God's desired target for His people may be reached. I can hear God saying now, "Well done good and Faithful Servant." May God continue to bless and keep you!

—Pastor Valencia Scott

INTRODUCTION

I HAVE A NEWS FLASH FOR YOU... I HOPE AND PRAY THAT you will give great consideration to what this book is telling you about something that is so valuable and important. Do you take the time to make sure that you are doing all you can to cherish, appreciate, and target your soul to reach the place where you want to spend eternity? In this book, I will endeavor to enlighten you about targeting your soul to meet our Lord and Savior in peace; therefore, allowing your soul to enter into eternal peace.

Your soul is regarded as the one thing you have, that you can only have one of. It is extremely critical that you take care of it and see that it will not be destroyed. The soul of man is who you truly are, also better regarded as the whole person. Your soul embodies your feelings, your personality, your passions, and your dreams. It is the identity of the person that cannot be defined materially, is separate from the body but seen through physical attributes.

Not only should your soul be important to you, but it is equally, if not more important, to God. The soul of man is the bride of Christ. Just as in the Garden of Eden before the fall of man, God still communes with man today, every day in fact. What a love affair God has with man's soul! How do we know that this is the case? It is found in Genesis 2:7, which declares, "And the Lord God formed man of the dust of the ground and breathed into his nostrils the breath of life, and man became a living soul."

Now, I know what you may be asking, "How does Genesis 2:7 show intimacy and unity between God and man?" Well, let's look a little deeper. Because this is such a personal encounter, one would have to notice that forming man from the dust of the ground would only show our frailty and temporary physical state. But God would do something even more supernatural: He would breathe His Spirit into this body formed out of dust, and through His Spirit a soul would be created and fused with the Spirit of God. It is important to understand that the spirit (breath of life) and the soul of man would be intertwined, but not inseparable. We would find this to be true when God would give a commandment to man with a consequence attached should man not obey that commandment. Genesis 2:16 and 17 says, "And the Lord God commanded the man, saying, of every tree of the garden thou may freely eat: But of the tree of the knowledge of good and evil, thou shalt not eat of it: for in the day that thou eat thereof thou shalt surely die." Following this commandment from God, the serpent deceptively told the woman that they would not surely die. The serpent didn't, however, explain to the woman that when God spoke of death, He wasn't speaking simply of physical death, but rather, He was referring to spiritual death.

The word "death" means "separation." As previously stated, there are two types of death:

1. Physical Death is when the soul of man departs from the

formed dust of the ground.

2. Spiritual Death is when the Spirit of God is separated from the soul of man.

I guess we all know what happened. But yes, it is true: Man did not necessarily die physically, but he suffered a spiritual death. This meant not only being removed from the Garden of Eden, but most of all, from the presence of God. This is by far the worst thing that could have happened to man for several reasons: not only did we lose out on being in the presence of God, but our souls lost eternal life. Without the Spirit of God connected to the souls of men, our souls have no eternal direction after physical death which, therefore, leaves us with death, both spiritual and eternal.

So how do we get back what we lost? How do we get back on target? Is Salvation enough? How can I feel that my soul is secure and that God won't turn me away? What is "my soul's target?"

> Note: Don't forget to consider the "Sit in Silence" (S.I.S.) Moments in this book, as they are a great time to reflect and ponder over statements and/or questions.

SECTION ONE
MY SOUL

CHAPTER ONE

ITS PURPOSE

FINDING YOUR "SOUL'S PURPOSE" IS SETTING UP YOUR SOUL to hit its target. So many people walk around aimlessly with no direction and with no outlook for the next moment in their lives. There's something about knowing and pursuing your purpose for living: it creates a drive, a sense of happiness (pursuit), a love for life, and a closeness with our Creator. David recognized that God's creation is not a haphazard event and that our Father didn't just throw some dust together and call it a man. Psalm 139:14 explains, "For I am fearfully (carefully) and wonderfully made: marvelous are thy works; and that my soul knows right well." God's careful attention to detail in making us and forming us reveals to us how much He loves us. At no time should we take any creation of God as a mistake or without purpose.

Take into account a child before he or she is born into this world. No one can control the growth and physical maturity of the child while it's in the womb of the mother. All the mother can do is be careful of how she takes care of her body and what she places inside her so that the child's growth will not be hindered. It is God who performs the miracle of making sure that a simple seed and egg grow into a child. God is so involved in everything that concerns man that He even knows the number of hairs that are on our heads. Not only does David recognize the handy work of God from without, but even more from within; the great work of a Majestic King to make us physically perfect and specifically shaped for His use. We should also be so excited that it shows from the inside out.

S.I.S: Never let anyone steal your self-worth or make you feel less than who God has made you to be. This is an assurance that no one can take away because God Himself made you special, and therefore formed you with purpose in mind.

Before we go any further, we must define the word "Purpose" and then see how it applies to the soul. For it would seem to me that many can't find their "soul's purpose" because they don't know what purpose is and how it applies to their lives.

"Purpose" in its own right has two literal meanings that I would love to focus on as it pertains to your "soul's target". The first definition for "purpose" is "the reason why something is done; it is your aim for accomplishing something." The next meaning is "the feeling of being determined to do or achieve something; which is the drive it takes to complete that which you have set out to accomplish."

So let's summarize it to make sure we have it: the word "purpose" means the reason why you want to accomplish something, then also having the drive and ambition to carry it through. (Example: His purpose for going to college was to obtain a degree, so he purposed in his heart that nothing would stop him). How powerful is this one word to set the order and direction of one's life on track? You may ask, "What does this have to do with targeting my soul?" I am glad you asked. If you are a person with a "Purpose Driven Soul" you have the greatest potential of fulfilling your destiny because you have the hope of reaching that target and every reason in the world to make sure you don't fail or quit. Quite frankly, if heaven is your target, identify your purpose for wanting to get there and purpose in your heart that nothing is going to stop you from accomplishing that goal. But you must put your all into it!

In my studying, there is another word that often accompanies the word "soul"; that word is "heart". The words "heart" and "soul" to me are like twins that are somewhat inseparable. It would even seem relevant that the heart is the very life of the soul. Just as the heart is the main function of the body's existence, it also gives life support to our very souls. The giving of your heart and soul to a purpose or a mission is the sign of a person who will not be deterred or removed from the course set before them. God even recognizes the unity of the powerful dual couple and would often require that the heart and soul align themselves in order to serve Him—that is to say, if He has your heart and soul, He has your all. For example, our heavenly Father isn't and has never been short on fulfilling His promises to us. Would we be far from reality if we were to say that God puts His heart and soul into everything He does? He does and provides this to man. Why? Because He has purposed to love us in spite of what we do and how we treat Him. Our Father purposed in His heart that He would give His life for the purpose of bringing us back into fellowship with Him, and this, in turn, would refocus the souls of those who believe in Christ and set them back on target.

Now, if God can give us His all (heart and soul) then He would also require nothing less from us. His desire for this closeness with us is expressed in Deuteronomy 11:13, which says, "And it shall come to pass, if ye shall obey diligently unto my commandments which I command you this day, to love the Lord your God, and to serve Him with all your heart and with all your soul..." This verse then continues to explain all of the promises He would fulfill that's connected to us giving our all. What makes this a joy is that God initiated the practice of giving one's all by always being there for the children of Israel, from Egypt to Canaan. Again, we find purpose and the soul of man wrapped up in God's eternal purpose.

I would have to derive from this that the purpose for my soul is to be wholly entrusted to a faithful God who has purposed in His heart that He will love us without limitation or reservation and would only ask for the same commitment of our hearts and souls to Him in return. Too simple, right? I believe this is achievable because we have a great example of this in our Lord and Savior, Jesus Christ. Christ understood the purpose of His coming and gave His all into fulfilling this purpose (or mission). Despite knowing that His mission would be filled with great struggle, Jesus would not be deterred; He yielded to His purpose. There is no greater fulfillment in life than knowing why God created you and seeking to fulfill that mission; than giving your heart and soul to the purpose for which you were designed since the world began.

There is one last thing I need you to understand about your "soul target" as it pertains to your purpose. As stated in the introduction, the soul is the life of man; it is everything you are; it cannot be camouflaged, faked, or misrepresented. That's why the Bible says, "Man looks on the outward appearance, but the Lord looks on the heart" (1 Samuel 16:7). Your soul's purpose must be fulfilled, and I pray that it will be. I want to encourage you to get on that road of purpose on purpose and don't stop until you have reached your "soul's target"!

CHAPTER ONE:
ITS PURPOSE
(WORK SECTION)

The word "purpose" has a dual meaning. In your own words, what does "purpose" mean to you and how does it help you stay focus:

_____

_____

_____

_____

_____

_____

_____

_____

_____

_____

_____

_____

_____

_____

Exercise: Name some characteristics of people you may know or see that seem to be walking around with no purpose for their lives:

1._____

2._____

3._____

4._____

5._____

According to Psalm 139:14, we are fearfully and wonderfully made. What other scriptural references could you use to support David's claim?

_____

_____

_____

_____

_____

How does knowing this help you with your walk and stay on target?

_____

_____

_____

_____

_____

Everyone has a purpose for being here. God does not waste His breath. What do you feel your purpose is?

_____

_____

_____

What are you doing to fulfill that purpose?

_____

_____

_____

_____

_____

Giving your all to the service of God and to the fulfillment of your purpose is God's requirement, what two things must align themselves as a show of your commitment to your purpose?

_____

_____

God is committed to His people and He gives His all. Just as a personal testimony to someone, write of a time when you know God was there for you, and you felt His committed love in your life. (Homework)

_____

_____

_____

_____

_____

_____

_____

_____

_____

_____

_____

_____

_____

_____

_____

Our Lord and Savior, Jesus Christ, came here on "purpose" for a "purpose". What does this mean to you? (Be sure to use the word "purpose" in both its forms)

_____

_____

_____

_____

_____

_____

_____

_____

_____

_____

_____

_____

_____

Another page has been provided for extended answers. Be sure to reference the sections letter and number for easy referencing (example (A1))

Additional Notes:

CHAPTER TWO

ITS IMPORTANCE

M ANY OF US EITHER OWN OR HAVE OWNED SEVERAL cars, homes, shoes and articles of clothing. We have lavished our lives with so many things—some things we put to good use and a lot of things we wasted. There is one thing that we will only have one of and must be vigilant about taking care of, one thing we should treat it better than gold: our souls. How important is your soul? Jesus clued us in and answered that question by asking us a question: In Mathew 16:26, Jesus asked, "For what is a man profited if he shall gain the whole world, and lose his own soul? Or what will a man give in exchange for his soul?" These are very thought-provoking questions asked by our Savior, which causes us to think about what we put before our own salvation. It would probably seem rhetorical to have asked such a question to some; but even now, that same question needs to be answered not through our words, but through our actions: our devotion and dedication.

S.I.S. - What takes priority in your life? What do you from pay more attention to your than Soul?

It is truly mind boggling to say the least that even God's children would take chances with something that is so valuable. Do we do this because we feel our sins are automatically blotted out due to our singing on praise teams, preaching in pulpits, and serving as Deacons and Ushers? It's one thing to not recognize you have a soul that must be saved from sin and reckless living, but to know that your soul is hanging in the balance and yet do nothing to secure it, that is just unwise. Consider that one day your soul will be required of you, and you will have to give an account for every deed done in this earthly body.

But why take such a chance? Who having gold in their possession will continue to put it in the hands of a thief? Yes, a thief! Picture your soul as something more valuable than gold—if you know the thief only wants to steal, kill and destroy, why you would ask him to hold and take care of your valuable possession, which is more valuable than gold? The Bible says in John 10:10, "…the thief comes not but for to steal, and to Kill, and to destroy…" Destroy what? Your soul, the one true thing you have of value. Let that be an eye opener for you: Satan has no interest in your stuff. We often attribute the loss of cars, houses, money and things to Satan and we want these things back, but in actuality, the devil does not want or need your stuff. Furthermore, if he is allowed to bother your stuff, it is with the intent to lure your soul into a trap, hoping that your soul is connected to the stuff and that you would want the stuff more than God. Unfortunately, we are waging war against the enemy for all the wrong reasons. God will restore our things/stuff when we focus on His kingdom and righteousness and focus on our soul's target (Mathew 6:33).

When we don't assess and monitor our actions, we are literally letting the thief in to take advantage of our souls. How many chances will you take before the thief's plan is carried out? But as Jesus continued in that verse, He completed that statement by saying, "I am come that they might have life, and that they might have it more abundantly." Jesus said He wants to give life to a soul that is headed for destruction and death. I'd choose abundant life for my soul over death any day. By doing so, I'd be choosing not to take any more chances with my soul and to not allow the thief (Satan) to manipulate me into thinking that this world is worth risking my soul for.

How important are souls and does one soul mean more to God than another? To God, all souls are of equal value; no soul's worth is greater than the other. It doesn't matter about your social status, economic status, titles, degrees or positions; all souls are the same in our Father's eyes. God even claimed ownership of the souls of men in Ezekiel 18:4 where He declared, "Behold, all souls are mine; as the soul of the son is mine: To express this universal love for all souls." John 3:16 says, "For God so love the world that He gave His only begotten Son, that whosoever would believe in Him, would have everlasting life." I believe the phrase "the world" consists of every living soul.

As found in Exodus 30:11-16, God required an offering from the Children of Israel: He required that all those who were 20 years and older to give half a shekel as an atonement for their souls. But here is the catch: Because no soul is more important than the other, God did not require the rich to give more, neither the poor to give less; all had to give the same because rich or poor, your soul has no status connected to it. So, are you saying that just because I preach, sing, evangelize, prophesy, speak in tongues, and have all these gifts that doesn't place my soul at the top of God's most valuable list? Yes. You are not special in God's eyes because you are gifted. Jesus paid one ransom for all souls; through this, you must see how important your soul is to Him and should be to you.

Sometimes, it seems as if we value the souls of others even more than our own. I often wonder why it seems at times like we are so ready to get others' souls on track but we neglect to take the same measures to ensure that we don't miss out on heaven. Yes, I know you may say "That is not me" or "I care more about my soul than I do others." Well, that's great, but I would like to ask you a few questions:

1. Have you ever sent your children to church while you stayed at home to cook, clean, catch up on the soap operas, wash your car, watch a game on television or just do something you found more important?

2. Have you ever gone to a family gathering and saw Uncle Bob doing something or heard that Cousin Lou was involved in something and you approached them to ask what in the world have they gotten themselves into while not acknowledging that you have been or are still caught up in some mess yourself that you haven't addressed?

3. Have you ever gone to your job and told somebody that Jesus saves and that God is a good God, but when things go wrong in your life, everyone gets cursed out and treated wrongly by you and you start acting unbecoming of a child of God?

You can't put others on target with their souls until you love your own soul enough to get on target and stay focus. It is interesting that Paul told the church in Philippians 2:12, "Wherefore, my beloved, as ye always obeyed, not as in my presence only, but now much more in my absence, work out your own salvation with fear and trembling." I believe understanding the importance of your soul is realizing that it is a 24 hour, 7 days a week, 365 days a year process to stay on target. Paul even said in 1 Corinthians 9:27, "But I keep under my body, and bring it into subjection; lest that by any means, when I have preached to others, I myself should be a castaway." Yes, we should be concerned about the souls of others, but don't focus on others without first adjusting your site and bringing your flesh and desires under subjection—lest we preach to others and our souls be lost.

The last example I want to use is the one of flying the friendly skies. I was struck by one of the instructions on a plane that explained what to do in case of an emergency: When the cabin loses pressure, you must first place the oxygen mask on yourself before you try to help someone else with theirs. I use to think that if my son or someone who may not be able to help themselves is sitting next me, it would make sense for me to help him first. But then I realized that the rationale behind those instructions is that you can't help save someone's life if you've lost your own. How important is your soul? It is the most important possession you have. It is your connection with the Spirit of God, and it is eternal. Do all that you can to save it!

CHAPTER TWO:
ITS IMPORTANCE
(WORK SECTION)

On a scale of 1 to 10, how often do you consider your soul on a day to day basis? (1 being not much at all; 10 being every day you consider your soul's importance.) This is for you, so be honest with yourself.

(1-10):_____

Why do you give yourself that rating?

_____
_____
_____
_____
_____

What do you put before your soul, if anything? Or just as a testimony to someone else, name something God has delivered you from that kept you from seeing how important your soul is.

_____
_____
_____
_____
_____
_____

_____

_____

_____

_____

Explain the ransom of souls (Exodus 30:11-16): (Homework)

_____

_____

_____

_____

_____

_____

_____

_____

_____

_____

_____

_____

_____

_____

Why is this Old Testament command no longer necessary?

_____

_____

_____

_____

_____

_____

_____

Your soul has to be the most important thing that you have.
It must be protected, because there is a thief that is waiting
to steal, kill, and destroy it. Name some things you can do
to take better care of your soul:

_____

_____

_____

_____

_____

_____

_____

_____

_____

_____

_____

_____

_____

Additional Notes

_____

_____

_____

_____

_____

_____

_____

_____

_____

_____

_____

_____

_____

_____

_____

_____

_____

_____

_____

_____

_____

_____

_____

_____

CHAPTER THREE

ITS CHARACTERISTICS

Your soul is that which expresses who you really are: you are a soul. Your soul is what God considers as the true you. I am so glad that Jesus came to save souls and not "clothes" ("Clothes" meaning anything we put on to cover up the parts of us that people can't see, and, in most cases, what we don't want others to see). One thing I noticed about many church services is that they are some of the biggest fashion shows in the world. All the fine suits, clothes, hats, and dresses are represented at these gatherings. But dressing up the outside cannot cover up the inside, and eventually your soul's condition will come shining through. "Soul Characteristics" are nothing to be ashamed of. It's the hiding of one's true self or attempt to be someone you are not that makes life harder and causes others to not be able to relate to you as an individual. Be a good representative of your own soul: if it's not you, then don't fake it; if it is you, then embrace it and make the best of it.

S.I.S. – What are some of your "soul characteristics" and how do they help or hurt your walk with Christ?

Soul-characteristics are truly exemplified by our God. The deep and intense feelings and emotions are not just feelings that we feel, but these are shared by our Father and were sent to us through His Son. Amazingly enough, Jesus was a partaker of every emotion and feeling that our souls are touched with today. Hebrews 4:15 says, "For we have not a high priest which cannot be touched with the feeling of our infirmities; but was on all points tempted like as we are, yet without sin." Jesus was fully connected with His soul and is now connected with our souls, and He cares about us so much because He knows and remembers just what He endured on this earth. He definitely understands hurt, pain, agony, joy, love, peace, sorrow, and other soul characteristics, some of which we will get into later.

You may ask again, "What do my soul's characteristics have to do with my soul's target?" Thanks again for asking. How you feel and what's important to you has everything to do with where you are going. Your soul embodies your passions and the things you desire. We are not just talking about the mundane things of life; no, these are things that you value in life. Think about it just for a second. Your valuable soul would have to hold certain things in high regard, or else you would accept whatever is thrown your way: any type of treatment, conversation or company that is presented. If you don't hold your soul to a high standard, you will be controlled by other influences, therefore getting your soul off track. Simply put: If you value your soul, you will value what you allow to affect it.

God's soul is seen through every part of His character—with Him being three persons in one. We see different
characteristics in all three, but all under the authority of
God. Through God the Father we see love and concern,
and yet, He is stern and unmovable in His commitment.
Through God the Son we see dedication to a purpose
through compassion and determination paired with obedience and sacrifice, and through God the Holy Spirit we see
gentleness and grace, and yet, power that yields miracles
and the fruit or attributes of the Father. God's soul is moved
and it causes Him to run to the rescue of the people He
loves.

What moves your soul? What pushes you to run,
respond, or reach out? These are the things that show the
true character of your soul. We would find many times in
Scripture where God was moved for the purpose of coming
to the aid of the Children of Israel. Judges 10:15-16 shows
us how once again, the Children of Israel returned to God
after doing evil in His sight. Isn't it amazing that, even despite the Israelites losing God's presence, they never lost His
heart? Take close notice of verse 16 of chapter 10 in Judges:
"And they put away the strange gods from them, and served
the Lord: and 'His Soul' was grieved (could no longer stand
their pain) for the misery of Israel." What an awesome King!
Even though we commit sins against God, He is still moves
when He hears our earnest cries and will come to our rescue. A definite characteristic of the soul is compassion that
reaches the heart.

What makes one soul cry out for another's? Why
does the soul of God reach out to the souls of men? Can
our souls tie into the souls of others' so much that we actually become one with them? The merging of souls can
only come through one means, and that is the "Covenant

of Love". Notice that I said the "Covenant" of Love; this is not just any type of love or love as you may think, the kind that is here today and gone tomorrow. When your soul is targeted to love, nothing and no one can come in between that; and this love cannot be broken. This love suffers long, is kind, envies not, vaunts not itself, is not puffed up, does not behave itself unseemly, seeks not its own, is not easily provoked, thinks no evil, rejoices not in iniquity, but rejoices in truth, bears all things, believes all things, hopes all things, endures all things; it never fails (1 Corinthians 13:4-8). This love is shown through God, who is love, and was proven by the gift of His Son—a gift given as a token of the Covenant of Love which could only express how much He really and truly loves us. This love cut to the very core of God's soul and went so deep that He created a plan to not only bring us back to Him, but to prove His love for us; and the only way He could do it and show how much we meant to Him was for Him to die for us.

The closest example that God could give us of the type of love He has for us is the institution of marriage. In a marriage it is said that two become one. We know that physically you cannot make two bodies become one, so what is being referred to as becoming one? You got it: the souls of the individuals become one, meaning that all that they do is in unity and the only way this bonding of souls can be broken is through death or the breaking of the Covenant Vow. A ring is given to represent the token of love and their unending covenant for as long as they both shall live. This is also why Paul, in 2 Corinthians, admonished us in chapter 6:14 not to be "unequally yoked together with unbelievers: For what fellowship has righteousness with unrighteousness, and what communion hath light with darkness?" This Soul Characteristic is the greatest because it is the very basis upon which God has established every commandment that keeps us on target.

One of the greatest biblical accounts of this "Covenant of Love" is found in 1 Samuel 18:1, which reveals a brotherly love that was so close it was regarded as being a soul knitting between David and Jonathan. The Bible says Jonathan loved David as he loved his own soul. What a love and joining of a heart and soul to another individual's. And let us not forget about the token of love. Verse 3 says, "...then Jonathan and David made a covenant, because he loved him as his own soul." Verse 4: "And Jonathan stripped himself of the robe that was upon him, and gave it to David, and his garment, even to his sword, and his bow, and his girdle." Undoubtedly, this covenant had to overcome challenges and situations. But when the covenant of love is in effect, the souls are joined and no problem is insurmountable. Does this sound familiar? Covenant love gives all!

Not only is a Targeted Soul compassionate and loving, but it also obtains a characteristic that is key to life itself: a "Patient Soul", which is a soul that is well able to handle the challenges of this life. This stands true for several reasons, and I would love to cover this for you if you have the patience. (Smile)

The first reason a patient soul is a soul on target is it takes patience to hit a target. A marksman's attempt to hit a target requires that they take the time to carefully aim, consider, and go through all of the techniques needed to hit their target and show that they are skillful at their craft. Truthfully, it doesn't take skill to be impatient, and impatience will never produce any skills; and in most cases, it won't bring any success. A patient soul breeds expectation, lives with hope, and walks by faith. The 62nd Psalm of David says, "Truly my soul waits upon God: from Him cometh my salvation." Yes, David, in essence, caught hold of something that would change his life. Notice this: When you exercise patience, you have conquered so many emotions that can potentially hinder you from being blessed, finding success, and moving forward in life. David said, Truly, I have a soul quality that is undeniable. Waiting on the Lord is a way of telling God that you expect help from no one else besides Him. So, I will just wait until my salvation or my Savior comes and rescues me. Nothing moves God like a child who will wait with patience for Him to show up. Waiting for God is like baking a cake: once you have in all the right ingredients, you put it in the oven and then it's out of your hands. It's up to the oven to do the rest, and all you can do is wait for the expected time that it will be finished. A targeted soul is patient and waits until the right time, the right place, and the right choices are made evident.

I use to hear the older saints say be careful when you ask God for more patience. I realize now why they said it: patience is a Soul Characteristic that is produced by going through actual trials and tribulations. Romans 5:3-4 says, "And not only so, but we glory in tribulations also: knowing that tribulations works patience; and patience, experience; and experience, hope." Now, this should make us look at the things we go through a little differently. God is using what we feel is hurtful, painful, and discomforting to give us something we need in order to reach heaven. "Patience" is working the experience we need to hit our soul's target; and that experience is what gives us the hope that we will one day hit our target and see our Savior! Glory to God!

The soul is filled with emotions, feelings and ambitions. But there is a characteristic of the soul that cannot be fulfilled by anything but its Creator. There is a natural thirst, a longing of the soul to be connected to and in communion with its Creator. Growing up, I would often hear the older people refer to a hole in the soul that could only be filled by Jesus. I now clearly understand what they were talking about. Whether it is recognized or not by us, I truly believe that every living soul is seeking for a greater fulfillment which can only be given by God. That is the reason why those of us who have allowed Jesus into our hearts can testify that that longing, that thirst within us has been quenched by the presence of an Almighty God through His Spirit.

One person who realized that God's presence in his life was the one thing he couldn't live without is David. David was in the Judean wilderness when he penned the 63rd Psalm: "O God, thou art my God; early will I seek thee: my soul thirst for thee, my flesh long for thee in a dry and thirsty land, where no water is; to see thy power and thy glory, so as I have seen thee in the sanctuary." I'm sure many of us can relate to what David was speaking of and can definitely say that at some point in our lives we have felt like we were in a dry and thirsty place. Being in sin is being in that place where our souls long for salvation, deliverance, and freedom. Jesus told the woman at the well that He could give living water and that she would never have to thirst again (John 4:14). After reading this story, it is evident that Jesus recognized that this woman's thirst for salvation was much greater than her physical thirst. We must also see that the world is thirsty for salvation. Just as we, who're saved, need that spiritual quenching, so do those who are still lost. Just look at the condition of the world who's trying to quench its thirst using immoral acts, violence and all types of evil doing, not realizing that the only thing needed is the living water given by Christ. I pray that the thirst of the wicked grows so overwhelming that they will run to the church, to those of us that have that water on the inside of us and ready to give it freely.

The last two characteristics of the soul that I want to bring your attention to are sorrow and joy. These are real feelings and real emotions, but not just on the surface; sorrow and joy cut to the very core of the soul. I know that at some point we have all felt the pain of sorrow. But understanding that sorrow is a feeling that comes from the very depths of the soul will also give us insight into to how God uses it to get our attention and even set us back on "target". God gets our attention with things like the loss of a loved one, the experience of seeing someone you truly love face struggles, and the agony of facing something you don't want to go through.

Yes, sorrow is inevitable. Jesus faced the agony and pain of sorrow several times in His ministry. Jesus' greatest sorrow came when He was about to face the cross; however, let's visit some other moments that caused Him to feel sorrow just before facing the cross. He had to tell His disciples that He was going to have to die, one of His disciples would betray Him, one of His disciples would deny Him, and all of the disciples would have to feel the sorrow of losing their Savior. Mathew 26:38 reads, "...then said he unto them, my soul is exceeding sorrowful even unto death: tarry ye here and watch with me." The Amplified Version says, "Then He said to them, my soul is very sad and deeply grieved, so that I am almost dying of sorrow." Wow! Even Jesus, before getting to the cross, felt like He was about to die from grief and sorrow.

Have you ever experienced so much sorrow that you thought you were going to die? Be completely honest and admit that you actually wanted to leave this world. There are not too many emotions that can cause you to want to take your life by your own hands. The only good thing about sorrow is that it does not last always. It may at the time seem like pain is all that matters. Here again we are encouraged through Psalm 30:5: "For His anger endure but a moment; in His favor is life: weeping may endure for a night, but joy cometh in the morning." This Psalm gives us a promise that even though sorrow comes, if we are able to endure it, we will experience the soul characteristic of joy.

A joyful soul is a soul at rest, at peace, and one that is satisfied by Christ. Real joy is knowing God and how much you mean to Him. Psalm 35:9 says, "And my soul shall be joyful in the Lord: it shall rejoice in His salvation." God will rescue His people from the chains of sorrow and give us His joy—the joy that the world can't give and the world can't take away. Need more confirmation of this? Psalm 126:5 says, "They that sow in tears shall reap in joy." In another instance, reaping the reward is greater than the agony of sowing. Even though joy and sorrow are Soul Characteristics, they both cannot exist at the same time; both have their times and seasons. But as a word to the wise and encouraging point: if you find yourself in a time of sorrow, hold on and look forward to the morning because joy is coming.

> S.I.S. – Do you agree or disagree with this statement: "The joy that follows sorry is far greater than the sorrow that is experienced."

CHAPTER THREE:
ITS CHARACTERISTICS
(WORK SECTION)

What are some characteristics about you that are recognizable and cannot be hidden? Explain how they affect your life, good and bad.

_____

_____

_____

_____

_____

_____

_____

_____

_____

_____

_____

What are things you may do or see others do to try to cover up who they really are?

_____

_____

_____

_____

_____

_____

_____

_____

_____

_____

_____

_____

_____

_____

Jesus was a partaker of every emotion, this is the reason His soul was and is still connected with the Souls of man (Hebrews 4:15); Research in scripture some of the emotions that Jesus faced while here on earth. Give scriptural references for what you find. (Homework)

_____

_____

_____

_____

_____

_____

_____

_____

_____

_____

_____

_____

We all go through several emotional highs and lows, some
have a great potential of deterring you from your soul's target. Name some emotional influences the devil use to get us
off target and explain how these work against you:

_____

_____

_____

_____

_____

_____

_____

_____

_____

_____

_____

_____

Compassion is a soul-characteristic: It is actually a soul-tie
to someone else that will cause you to feel what someone
else is feeling and cause you to react or move on their be-
half. Judges 10:15-16 is one instance of God's compassion
on Israel. Find in Scripture two other times where God's
soul-characteristic of compassion was shown in place of His
judgement and explain what you find. (Homework)

_____

_____

_____

_____

_____

_____

_____

_____

_____

_____

_____

_____

_____

_____

_____

_____

_____

_____

_____

_____

Another Soul characteristic is "Love": explain the "Covenant of Love" by giving detailed definitions for the words "covenant" and "love". Finish by giving a personal testimony of this type of love and how it has affected your life.

_____

_____

_____

_____

_____

_____

_____

Continue with the "Covenant of Love" (C6)

_____

_____

_____

_____

_____

_____

_____

_____

_____

_____

_____

_____

_____

Read 2 Corinthians 6:14: How does this passage keep us on target and/or get us off target if not obeyed?

_____

_____

_____

_____

_____

_____

_____

_____

_____

_____

_____

_____

_____

The story of David and Johnathan is so unique in that they were closely Soul knitted (1 Samuel 18:1) The Covenant of Love is recognized from God to man, and from husband and wife, but is hardly recognized through friendships. Think of a covenant of love relationship you have had with someone. What made this bond so tight?

_____

_____

_____

_____
_____
_____
_____
_____
_____
_____
_____
_____
_____
_____

A Patient Soul is a targeted soul (Psalm 62). Explain a circumstance when you had to exercise patience in order to maintain your soul's target:

_____
_____
_____
_____
_____
_____
_____
_____
_____
_____
_____

_____

_____

_____

_____

_____

_____

The hunger and thirst for a living God is real, once you have tasted of how good God is, your soul begins to want more and more (Psalm 63). In your own words and through experience, explain what this thirst does in you and what do you do to quench that thirst for God.

_____

_____

_____

_____

_____

_____

_____

_____

_____

_____

Joy and sorrow are two very real soul-characteristics and will at some point effect every living soul. They are the exact equal opposites of each other and can measure in great intensity. Talk about a time of sorrow that you have faced, and what did it take to get back to that place of joy, or in other words, when did your morning come? (Psalm 30:5)

_____

_____

_____

_____

_____

_____

_____

_____

_____

_____

_____

_____

_____

Additional Notes

_____

_____

_____

_____

_____

CHAPTER THREE: ITS CHARACTERISTICS

_____

_____

_____

_____

_____

_____

_____

_____

_____

_____

_____

_____

_____

_____

_____

_____

_____

_____

_____

_____

_____

_____

_____

_____

CHAPTER FOUR

ITS DESTINATION

I'M NOT SURE HOW MANY PEOPLE HAVE TOLD YOU THAT the soul doesn't go anywhere after you die, or that it re-incarnates after death, or that there is some holding place between heaven and hell, or that everybody goes to heaven, etc. But the Bible makes it specifically clear regarding what happens to the soul after it departs from the physical body, and the Bible also makes is crystal clear that it is totally up to the individual where their soul ends up after they die. In this section, we will discuss the only two destinations that exist for your soul once you die. These two destinations are the final targets for your soul. Unfortunately, because of the nature of man, one option (target) is much easier to hit than the other. But make no mistake: You will hit one of these eternal targets after you die. Have you ever played darts or practiced archery? How difficult is it to hit the red circle in the middle? And how much concentration is involved in doing so? Well, spiritually, it's the same concept. Let's take a look at the first of the two destinations: hell.

Hell is a literal place of punishment for the wicked after death. It is also referred to as a state of being or place of discomfort before physical death. In the Hebrew Bible, it is call it Sheol, and the Greeks called it Hades. The most important thing to understand about hell is that it is not where God dwells. The definition of hell explains that this place is a state of being and also a physical place. Another note is that the state of being could and should be temporary, but the actual physical place is eternal. In other words, you may be going through hell right now, but don't go to hell. We go through tormenting and tortuous situations. There are several examples in the Bible where the writers considered their current states to be hellish experiences. There is one thing about hell that is consistently true: Be it a state of being or a physical place, if a person ends up in hell it is because they chose sin and disobedience over obeying the word of God. David described experiencing great sorrows and confrontations from enemies as a hellish experience. Jonah, while in the belly of a fish, stated, "Out of the belly of hell cried I…" He called his experience hell because of the torment that he was going through, but he was going through it because of his disobedience.

If a temporary state of hell is that bad, one could only imagine how bad the eternal, physical place is. I want you to consider the thought so you will aim your soul in the opposite direction and avoid this place. The temporary state is nowhere near as bad as the eternal place. The Bible says the physical hell will be filled with weeping and gnashing of teeth. The eternal hell is the destination for souls that have been disconnected from the Spirit of God. Jesus told a story in Luke 16:23 about a beggar and a rich man in which He gave a very explicit description of the torture and pain the rich man would spend eternity going through and would never escape due to going to hell. Jesus would also give a warning in Luke 12:5 saying, "But I will forewarn you whom ye shall fear: fear Him, which after he hath killed hath power to cast into hell; yea, I say unto you, Fear Him." There used to be a time when hell was talked about a lot; it was like a scared straight program for sinners and believers. But now it's either not talked about at all or the word has been used so much out of context that even the thought of hell has been watered down. Don't get it twisted: hell is real, and it is not as some people describe who have watered it down. The pain, torture, and agony of hell is still just as bad as when it was originally created, and it always will be. Again, Jesus gave us several descriptions of hell revealing to us why we should desire to avoid this place. In Mark chapter 9, verses 43, 45, and 47, Jesus said, "If your hand, foot or eye offend you, then it would be better to lose it and go into the Kingdom of God with one that to go to hell." In other words, it is better to go through hurt, pain, and self-denial down here on earth than to go to hell where there is no end to the hurt and pain. So many people take for granted what the Bible says about hell; and yet, they're heading there and will end up wishing they would have just listened and been obedient to the word of God.

"But how could a loving God allow this to be?" you ask. I'm glad you asked. Take into consideration all that our loving God has endured while on this earth: pain, anguish, bruised, beaten, mocked, being spat upon, nailed, pierced in His side with a spear, and more. But for what? Just so that He could develop a relationship with us. He paid the ultimate price, which was to die a horrible and excruciatingly painful death just to prove His love for us. Furthermore, consider how it makes the Creator feel when His own creation rejects Him in order to do their own thing and indulge in sinful ways and activities. We serve a jealous God who took His time to make us for Himself, and to be connected to anything else but Him is an insult to Him. When considering these things, it shouldn't be difficult to understand that there is a punishment in the form of eternal separation from God for those who choose to be disobedient and continue in their sinful and selfish ways. God simply will not tolerate for long those who live and practice sin and disobedience. His judgement is sure, and will come. 2 Peter 2:1-9 further reveals to us that if God would judge even the angels and destroy the world with a great flood, then it shouldn't be unimaginable that there is an eternal judgement for sinners: hell.

There is one last thing about hell that I have to tell you—and trust me, it doesn't get any better. Even hell is not the final judgment for those who choose sin and selfishness over God's way. Revelations 20:11-15 says, "And I saw a great white throne, and him that sat on it, from whose face the earth and the heaven fled away; and there was found no place for them. And I saw the dead, small and great stand before God; and the books were opened: and another book was opened which is the book of life: and the dead were judged out of those things which were written in the books, according to their works. And the sea gave up the dead which were in it; and death and hell delivered up the dead which were in them: and they were judged every man according to their works. And Death and hell were cast into the lake of fire." This is known as the second death. "And whosoever was not found written in the book of life was cast into the lake of fire". A terrible end to what was already a sad story. The great thing is this: the fact you are able to read about hell means you still have a chance to aim for heaven…and avoid hell altogether.

The target for the Believer is heaven; that is our home; it is our promise from God; it is where we strive to live, to make it to some day; this is the dwelling place of our Creator, our Father, and our Lord and Savior, Jesus Christ. It should be safe to say that if you consider everything it takes to go to hell and do the opposite, you will definitely hit the target of heaven. First of all, salvation is required to hit this target; and to be honest, I believe that this is the easy part. Romans 10:9 says, "If thou shalt confess with thy mouth the Lord Jesus, and shalt believe in thine heart that God hath raised Him from the dead, thou shalt be saved." Simple, right? Well, that's just the beginning of your Christian journey to heaven. On the road to heaven you must stay focused, occasionally re-focus (repent), and remain on target. It would be misleading for me to say it is a cake walk making it into heaven. This is why Jesus talked about self-denial. Not only will you face outside troubles, but just getting yourself to stay on target is hard enough. 1 Peter 4:17 and 18 says, "For the time is come that judgement must begin at the house of God: and if it first begin at us, what shall the end be of them that obey not the gospel of God? And if the righteous scarcely be saved, where shall the ungodly and the sinner appear?" The part I really want to emphasize is the fact that the righteous will "scarcely" make it in. I don't believe Peter was writing this to discourage Believers; he was writing this to encourage us to stay focused and know that heaven is worth fighting for.

With that being said, let's explore this wonderful place where, according to Revelation 21:12-14, the throne of God dwells. The Book of Revelation describes heaven as a place that has pure golden streets and gates made of pearl, and where there is no night. And for those of us that might never own a mansion down here, Jesus says in John 14:2,

"In my Father's house are many mansions: if it were not so, I would have told you. I go to prepare a place for you." A mansion? Prepared by Christ? Just for me? I have to hit this target!

But that's not even the best part. Heaven is the exact opposite of hell (Remember: the Bible describes hell as a place of hurt, pain, and torment). Regarding heaven, Revelation 21:4-5 tells us, "And God shall wipe away all tears from their eyes; and there shall be no more death, neither sorrow, nor crying, neither shall there be any more pain: the former things are passed away. And he that sat upon the throne said, Behold, I make all things new. And he said unto me (John) Write: for these words are true and faithful." Heaven should be our target. I don't want to go through hell on earth and then die and end up in hell forever. No thank you! I choose to aim for heaven where there will not exist the problems we have to face down here on earth.

The blessing of heaven does not come to all. Let's go back to Revelation one last time to see who inherits the blessing. Revelation 22:14 says, "Blessed are they that do His commandments that they may have right to the tree of life, and may enter in through the gates into the city." God's desire is for us to join Him and rejoice with Him in heaven, but we must keep heaven as our goal and stay focused.

S.I.S. – Even if one is unsure of what happens after death (you won't live forever), why take a chance and not make heaven your target, your goal?

62

CHAPTER FOUR:
ITS DESTINATION
(WORK SECTION)

Just out of curiosity what are some things you have heard happens to a person when they die?

_____

_____

_____

_____

_____

_____

_____

_____

Your soul can spend eternity in one of two places. Where and in your own words why would you prefer one over the other?

_____

_____

_____

_____

_____

_____

_____

_____

_____

_____

_____

_____

The Scriptures define those that will not see the kingdom of God. Make as detail of a list as you can of the acts of sin that will cause one not make it into the Kingdom using scriptural references:

_____

_____

_____

_____

_____

_____

_____

_____

_____

_____

_____

_____

_____

Hell is also defined as a state of being. Have you ever been in a situation that you felt was a hell type situation? What was the outcome and did it cause you move toward a heavenly focus, away from or nothing at all?

_____

_____

_____

_____

_____

_____

_____

_____

_____

_____

_____

_____

_____

_____

_____

Read Luke 16:19-31. This is an awesome account of not only the contrast between heaven and hell, but also the realistic choices of life and death. (Study this for discussion)

How do you feel about the topic of hell, and is this place losing conviction because of the lack of conversation or misuse of the word?

_____

_____

_____

_____

_____

_____

_____

_____

_____

_____

_____

_____

_____

_____

Do you know of someone who feels like they will make it to heaven regardless of the things they do? What do you see as sin in their lives?

_____

_____

_____

_____

_____

_____

How do you feel about 1 Peter 4:17-18? Discuss this scripture in detail in order to pull out points that will benefit the church and our process in targeting heaven. (Homework)

What is the most exciting thing about heaven to you? Why?

_____
_____
_____
_____
_____
_____
_____
_____
_____
_____
_____
_____

How does Revelations 21:4-5 encourage you personally and causes you to stay on target?

_____
_____
_____
_____
_____
_____
_____
_____
_____

_____
_____
_____
_____
_____
_____
_____
_____
_____
_____
_____
_____

Additional Notes

_____
_____
_____
_____
_____
_____
_____
_____
_____
_____
_____
_____
_____

SECTION TWO
GOD'S DESIGN

CHAPTER FIVE

PURPOSE IN CREATION

WHY AM I HERE AND WHY WAS I CREATED? THESE ARE questions that plague the minds of many; and yet, will still exist not getting a full answer. I'm also sure that you have heard many answers to that question, some of which may be right. If I may, I would like to take a moment and provide an answer to those who might still be a little unsettled as to why God created you. In order for us to get the answer we must go back to the beginning of the creation of man. Genesis 2:7 says, "And the Lord God formed man of the dust of the ground and breathed into his nostrils the breath of life; and man became a living soul." I pointed out this scripture because not only does it reveal the intimacy between God and man, but it reveals to us that God created man for a purpose, and only through becoming intimate with God can we discover our purposes.

It has always been God's intention to have a relationship with His creation. I have come to this understanding after years of wondering why God would create man and allow over time so much to happen, including our disobedience, turning our backs on Him, and so much more; and despite all we've done, God never gave up on the purpose for which He created us. God went through drastic measures just to prove His love for us and how much He desires a relationship with us. Picture this: The Bible says, "God is love" (1 John 4:8 and 16). What is love if there is no one to love and if you cannot prove it? One of the main purposes that we were created is so that a God, who is love, would have something, or, in our case, someone to love. His purpose for creating us became evident as He became wrong for our right, he became guilty for our innocence, love for our hatred, etc. All this for love and relationship.

No other creation can hold the heart of God so dearly and no other creation does God hold so dearly and give His heart to as he does with mankind. This is why it is important to know that you were created with a purpose in mind. Divine purpose is a very important concept to grab hold of. Your purpose was predestined by God from the beginning of time.

When considering your soul's target, it is crucial that you remember God created a plan for your soul and also that will have to give an account for everything that you do when Christ returns to retrieve you unto Himself. Let's visit someone who God revealed his purpose to, letting him know he had a purpose even before he was born.

Jeremiah 1:4-5 says, "Then the word of the Lord came unto me, saying, before I formed thee in the belly I knew thee; and before thou came forth out of the womb I sanctified thee, and I ordained thee a prophet unto the nations." This scripture captivates my heart every time I read it. God spoke to Jeremiah just like He speaks to us today and told him: Jeremiah, you are special to me. Notice that

God formed Jeremiah with the understanding that Jeremiah would be obedient to His word (foreknowledge), then God said that He sanctified and ordained him to be a prophet to the nations (predestination).

All souls do not have the same purposes in creation. That's why God is so awesome. He created us differently and designed that we all have different walks of life—some similar, but definitely different; and yet, there is one commonality, which is this: we were made, designed, and created by God. God created the world by design, and by design He created the balance of mankind. Creation and its purpose presents the presence of both good and evil. God did not create evil, but He orchestrates it and uses it to make us better. If we did not have struggles, then how often would we get on our knees? Truth be told, it's the good and the bad that keeps us focused and helps us to recognize the need to keep our souls on target.

Now that we have just established how important you are to God and how greatly He desires to have a relationship with you, let's explore this further. God created us for the sole purpose of establishing a relationship with us. Even still, there are some things that can cause us to make decisions that could impact our lives forever. Even after being in church all of your life, singing in the choir, playing instruments, shouting and dancing all over the building, and even preaching in the pulpit, you can still miss out on the most important part of the Christian walk. The part that we get right is religion, but the part that we often miss out on is what God desires the most: relationship. I sometimes wonder, if no one ever taught us how to act in church, how we would serve God? How would our praise be expressed? How would we express to God how much we love Him? What would our worship look and where would it come from?

Remember that your soul is the very embodiment of everything that means something to you. God created your soul so that he can recognize you and you can recognize yourself. With that being said, there is one part of you that you can really trust, be it in right or in wrong: Have you ever just had that feeling about something and just knew that things were not right, or something wasn't quite the way it appeared?

God created your soul to be keen and aware of your surroundings and to be able to discern certain atmospheres. Your soul, along with the presence of God, gives you an even more heightened sense of discernment. The Spirit of God, fused with our souls, gives us the supernatural ability to see what's not there, hear what's not spoken, and stand boldly in the power of God—working miracles, signs, and wonders. Believe it not, we were created to do supernatural things on this earth. That's why Jesus told His disciples that they would do greater works than what He did, but not until the Holy Spirit would be sent to them (which occurred on the day of Pentecost). Acts 1:8 says, "But ye shall receive power after that the Holy Ghost is come upon you: and ye shall be witnesses unto me both in Jerusalem, and in Judaea, and in Samaria, and unto the uttermost part of the earth."

It was always the plan of God to return us back in a right status with Him and help us to not be feeble with no direction but to be powerful, creative, and pleasing to our Maker. So, the question still remains: Why are we not walking in the God-given authority and power we so rightfully possess as Believers? May I submit a thought to those of us that believe: If you truly yearn to see the power of God operate in your life, then yearn even more to set your soul on target with God's plan for your life. The power of God is manifested in the life of a yielded soul.

The final thought I want to expound on regarding the soul's purpose in creation is where the soul actually belongs. Because we were created to be in perfect relationship with God, it would only seem reasonable to suggest that our souls belong to God and in His presence. Our souls were innately given the desire to seek for someone greater than ourselves. This is why even the most stubborn non-Believers at least recognize that there is a higher power existing and watching over the existence of man. The soul, therefore, seeks to fulfill this emptiness with other things and other people.

Psalm 42 greatly reveals to us the natural yearning of our souls to be in the presence of our Creator. It reads, "As the hart pants after the water brooks, so pants my soul after thee, O God. My soul Thirst for God, for the living God: when shall I come and appear before God?" These two verses expresses the writer's desire to be in the presence of God and in the house of God. This suggests that being in the presence of God brought peace to the writer's soul. That being said, this is the purpose for the creation of our souls: to be in the presence of God. Wow!

The Bible says, "Thou wilt show me the path of life: in Thy presence is the fullness of joy, at thy right hand there are pleasures for evermore" (Psalm 16:11). You can probably relate to the writer of Psalm 42. How do you feel when you go into the house of God? Doesn't it feel like all the burdens are lifted and that you can stay in that place forever? If so, it is because that's where the soul was designed to be. Our souls should never feel comfortable in hostile, sinful, and outrageous environments and atmospheres. Realistically, who wants to be in a place where their soul is uneasy? Remember what I said earlier: Because the Spirit of God has been fused with your souls, we can discern certain atmospheres spiritually; this is also why we, as true Believers, can't get comfortable around certain things and people. This is also why we have such a strong desire to see lives changed and chains and bounds broken off of people's lives. Yes, everywhere we go we should be creating an atmosphere that God will be pleased to dwell within and one that our souls can be comfortable in.

I want to end this segment by asking one question: Is your soul comfortable in the places where you spend the most time and around the people you spend the most time with? These maybe places you can't leave right away (i.e. jobs, homes, churches) and people who you can't just walk away from (i.e. family, loved ones, church members, co-workers). So, it is important to realize that if you can't change these things, change the atmosphere around these things. Remember the power you possess and use it to create a certain setting. As a point of reference, remember that you also have the power to create a hostile atmosphere; so use what you have wisely. The devil himself can't dwell in an atmosphere that has been prepared for the presence of God. We were purposely created to build a kingdom atmosphere on earth, one that mimics the atmosphere in heaven.

CHAPTER FIVE:
PURPOSE IN CREATION
(WORK SECTION)

We were created out of Love and because of Love. No other creation has or can have the relationship with God that man has and God created us for that reason. Why do you think God wanted to create man and are we fulfilling His expectation in creation?

_____

_____

_____

_____

_____

_____

_____

_____

_____

_____

_____

_____

_____

_____

_____

_____

_____

_____

_____

_____

Jeremiah 1:4-5: In the testimony of Jeremiah, God spoke
to him and told him he knew Jeremiah before he was in his
mother's womb. God would define two elements of His de-
ity in this verse. What are the meanings of these two word?
(Homework)

Foreknowledge:_____

_____

_____

_____

Predestination:_____

_____

_____

_____

Contrast "religion" and "relationship". How are they different and how are they the same, and where does your life fall
in at and why?

Answers:

_____

_____

_____

_____

_____

_____

_____

_____

_____

_____

_____

_____

_____

_____

_____

_____

_____

_____

_____

_____

A targeted soul is one that has the Spirit of God fused and knitted with it; this also gives to man supernatural gifts from the Spirit. Name two of the gifts given by the Spirit and how they help you stay on target.

_____

_____

_____

_____

_____

_____

_____

God's purpose in designing man was to love us into companionship, never to leave us. His presence would give us a fulfillment that nothing in this life can. Explain what the presence of God does for you especially in the times of hurt, sorrow, and disappointment (Psalm 16:11):

_____

_____

_____

_____

_____

_____

_____

_____

_____

Talk about a place where your soul has been uncomfortable, the atmosphere around you was unsettling to you: What did you do to change the atmosphere if anything?

_____

_____

_____

_____

_____

_____

_____

_____

_____

_____

_____

_____

Additional Notes

_____

_____

_____

_____

_____

_____

_____

_____

_____

_____

_____

_____

_____

_____

_____

_____

_____

_____

CHAPTER SIX

A DISCONNECTED SOUL

HAVE YOU EVER BEEN IN A PLACE WHERE YOU DIDN'T know where you were or how to get where you were going? You were lost with no GPS and no directions, or the directions you had weren't getting you where you wanted to be. This is one of the worst feelings anyone could ever experience; many people start to get frustrated, anxious, and even discouraged. Take that same feeling and apply it to a soul that is disconnected from the Spirit of God. Without God's Spirit leading and guiding us, we are lost with no direction and no stability; therefore, the soul gets agitated, restless, and looks for some type of direction.

If you examine the Bible from Genesis to Revelation, one of the main themes that it vividly points out to the Believer is that we will do wrong. As a matter of fact, Paul even pointed out in Romans chapter 7 that every time he chose to do right, evil was always present with him. Paul went on to carefully describe the things that he saw in himself and the components that played a great part in the decisions he made. Between chapters 7 and 8, Paul mentioned four laws that I believe we should always be aware of. These are key factors in targeting our souls for success:

1. The Laws of God- (7:22) Obedience to the Word of God; the innate feeling to do what is right and know you are in the will of God.
2. The Law of Sin- (7:21, 23) The law that was enacted by the disobedience of man in the garden. Therefore establishing that all men would be born in sin and shape in iniquity with propensity to commit sinful acts.
3. The Law of the Mind- (7:23) The very conscious of what is right and what is wrong, with the freedom to choose either.
4. The Law of the Spirit- (8:1) The actual Spirit of God sent to live on the inside of man to aid in directing, strengthen and keep us in the will of God.

The setup here is quite simple and relatable: It would take an evil mind to not at least want to adhere to the laws of God; and even when we do sin, it's shouldn't feel comfortable. Therefore, the Law of the Mind is aware and conscious of what is right and wrong and will naturally put up a fight against committing transgressions against what God has established as lawful. Unfortunately, because of our sinful nature we are born with, there is a strong desire to commit that which is unlawful because it feels pleasurable. God, due to His mercy and love for the souls of men, provided for us the only solution for dealing with the natural desire to sin, which is Himself. The only way that we can even stand a chance against our sinful natures is for God to come and provide to us Himself, drawing us closer to Himself. So, while sin bonds with our flesh, the Spirit of God bonds with our souls.

A soul that's disconnected from God cannot please God and will never reach heaven. Jesus said in John 16:13, "Howbeit when He, the Spirit of truth, is come, He will guide you into all truth; but whatsoever He shall hear, that shall He speak: and He will show you things to come." Now, if it takes the Spirit of Truth to lead us into all truth, then without God we will not be able to find truth and our sinful flesh will always lead us into lies. And our minds (imagination) will conjured up a reason to believe lies instead of obeying the truth. We see this every day in the lives of those who claim to know God but deny His power, wisdom, and righteousness. Some even claim to have God's presence in their lives, but live in sin and even claim that God is okay with them being the way they are. Anyone with the Spirit of God dwelling on the inside of them will never declare that the homosexual and lesbian life styles are right and that God made them that way, especially when God's Word clearly says that these sins, along with so many others, are worthy of death (Romans 1:26-32). (I will cover this later.) This is a judgement that only God can carry out. No man has that power or authority.

A soul disconnected from God is in a dangerous place, and this is definitely not God's desire for our lives. What good is an electrical appliance when it is disconnected from the power source? If you think that you are truly living life, and yet, you are disconnected from God and His divine plan for you and your soul is not targeted to reach the Kingdom of heaven, then you are being deceived by Satan.

As much as God loves the souls of men, He will not settle for second place in our hearts to anything or anyone. All souls belong to God; that much we have established. But Jesus picks it up again in Mathew 10:28 saying, "And fear not them which kill the body, but are not able to kill the soul: but rather fear Him which is able to destroy both soul and body in hell." Let's try this again: A soul that's not aimed at the target of heaven, one that is disconnected from the Spirit of God, only has one destination in eternity—yes, and you guessed it right: HELL!

We don't talk much about Hell. I understand. People would rather avoid the subject of hell rather than avoid the place. Jesus put it bluntly and straightforward when He said God has the power and the authority to send a disconnected soul to HELL. That may not seem right, but let's just think about this for a second: anything that is made is made under the authority of its creator. So, you have two types of non-Believers: the first is a person that neglects or outright resists the existence, presence, and authority of Almighty God; the second is a person that knows about the power of God, and yet, chooses to take their lives in their own hands—never targeting heaven, but focusing on the things of this world; and therefore, by default, they've chosen to target HELL.

Consider life as Jesus described it in John 5:1-8: Jesus is the vine and we are the branches. It is well known that a branch separated (disconnected) from its source of nourishment will eventually dry up and wither away. Each day that we stay disconnected from the Father we wither away slowly until we are good for nothing but to be thrown into the fire and burned. The importance of staying connected cannot be expressed any better than this and is really brought home in verse 5, which says, "I am the vine, ye are the branches: He that abide in me, and I in Him, the same shall bring forth much fruit: for without me ye can do nothing." Whoa! Jesus laid it all on the line with that statement. We can't do anything without Him, and whatever we are doing without Him will amount to nothing.

> S.I.S. – Just a thought: I would not want to live my whole life thinking that I'm doing something while disconnected from the Spirit of God, and then all that I do is burned up and not even considered as a testament of my life.

The targeting of your soul is very important, and you definitely should not take your soul for granted. Knowing that a disconnected soul has no direction should prompt you to find the Spirit of God who is the only one that can provide direction in life.

CHAPTER SIX:
A DISCONNECTED SOUL
(WORK SECTION)

A disconnected soul is one that is separated from the presence of the Holy Spirit. We have all been there and are born in it. Contrast the difference in how you felt separated from the Spirit of God to being connected:

_____

_____

_____

_____

_____

_____

_____

_____

_____

_____

_____

Romans 7:15-25 and chapter 8:1 explains the struggle of a connected soul struggling because of the laws listed. How do you see these laws play a part of life? (Homework)

The Law of God (7-22): _____

_____

_____
_____
_____
_____
_____

The Law of Sin (7:21,23): _____

_____
_____
_____
_____
_____

The Law of the Mind (7:23):

_____
_____
_____
_____
_____

The Law of the Spirit (8:1):

_____
_____
_____
_____

_____

_____

John 16:13. According to the study so far and this scripture, explain why a disconnected soul will not hit the heavenly target:

_____

_____

_____

_____

_____

_____

_____

_____

_____

_____

When it comes to "hell" people would rather avoid the conversation rather than avoid the place. Why is the conversation about "hell" not discussed that much in churches with or amongst the people of God and sinners?

_____

_____

_____

_____

_____

_____

_____

_____

_____

Why do you feel it is important for 'You" not to lose your connection with Christ?

_____

_____

_____

_____

_____

_____

_____

Additional Notes

_____

_____

_____

_____

_____

_____

_____

_____

_____

_____

_____
_____
_____
_____
_____
_____
_____
_____
_____
_____
_____
_____
_____
_____
_____
_____
_____
_____
_____
_____
_____
_____
_____
_____
_____

CHAPTER SEVEN
A CONNECTED SOUL

"INCLINE YOUR EAR, AND COME UNTO ME: HEAR, AND your soul shall live; and I will make an everlasting covenant with you, even the sure mercies of David" (Isaiah 55:3). One of the worst feelings in the world is to be disconnected spiritually from the Spirit of God. There is no greater feeling than to have your soul connected or reconnected to God. There is a feeling of security and comfort in knowing that you are in the arms of the Savior. I can truly relate to the wonderful hymn "Amazing Grace" where the writer penned the words, "I once was lost, but now I'm found." A reconnected soul is not just the Believer who once turned his back on the faith and has since returned, but we who are saved are all reconnected souls. We were all once living our lives as sinners but are now saved by grace.

Imagine a child in the womb of its mother with the umbilical cord connected to its belly. First off, the umbilical cord connects the mother with her child, and through this connection the mother is able to provide the child with blood rich in oxygen and nutrients while other vessels return deoxygenated blood and waste products such as carbon dioxide from the baby to the placenta. So, as you may already know, it's not just being inside the mother that is sustaining the life of the child, but it's actually being connected to the mother that gives life to the child. That's the way the Spirit of God is connected to our souls. Without God's Spirit we cannot receive the spiritual life sustaining nutrients that we need; and not only that, but there is no filtering system to rid us of the sin in our life that will in-turn produce death spiritually. It is through this connection that our blessings flow and God manifests Himself to be who He is in our lives. We are given all things as pertaining to life, health, and strength, and the power we need to come through at the expected time of our delivery.

Let's continue on with the benefits of being connected spiritually to God. Not only do we receive spiritual benefits from being connected to God, but we also receive physical, tangible benefits as well. I must approach this area very carefully because sometimes we think that being connected to God is just professing to know Him. The Father is requiring more of us than simply gaining knowledge about Him, or a simple profession of faith in order to receive Jesus Christ as our Savior. The Father is requiring that we walk in obedience to His Word and commandments. Jesus, in John 14:15, said, "If you love me, keep my commandments." We established that love is a soul attribute in its true form; therefore, the connection between love and obedience is important to God. Jesus said "If" as if to indicate that He knows whether or not you love Him due to your living and keeping the Word of God. A connected soul recognizes the importance of following Jesus' instructions. This is the key that God gives His people in order for us to see His blessings overtake our lives.

How important is obedience to God's Word? Let's find out from Deuteronomy 30:1-2: "And it shall come to pass, when all these things are come upon thee, the blessing and the curse, which I have set before thee, and thou shalt call them in mind among all the nations, whither the Lord thy God hath driven thee, And shalt return unto the Lord thy God, and shalt obey His voice according to all that I command thee this day; thou and thy children, with all thine heart and with all thy soul." The consequences of being disconnected and the rewards of being connected are pointed out in this particular scripture. The choice of obedience and disobedience, blessings and curses, are spelled out here. In essence, God is saying this: 'I set before you options, now you choose to connect to me or remain disconnected from me.' We are disconnected from God through our decision to disobey His Word.

God loves us so much He can't stand the thought of us continuing to neglect a relationship with Him simply because we find obedience to His Word taxing and boring. That's actually more of a human characteristic. We should be so thankful that God made a way for the door of redemption to swing on open to us. All we have to do to come out of disobedience is to confess, repent, and turn back to God. Doing this will put us back in a blessed place and remove the disconnect charge that was place on our souls.

There are so many ways that God, through His Spirit, reaches out to us in order to establish a close connection to us. The written Word of God, which is our spiritual handbook, is His main communication source. We hear God's Word through preachers and ministers, prophets and pastors, and through the wise counsel of senior and seasoned saints; and yet, there is one communication method that God uses that I believe we ignore the most: even after all of the preaching, teaching, prophesying, and sound wisdom, there is yet the nudging of that still small voice that speaks to our souls and tries to give us direction (review Hebrews 3:7,8). But listening is the key, and learning how to suppress our own selfish desires is the hard part. Sometimes we act as if we are either hard of hearing or just plain old stubborn. God has been speaking for generations, but we mostly ignore Him. Unfortunately, just like in the times of old, this has caused us to miss out on so many blessings and opportunities to do the work of the Lord in an effective and powerful way.

The story of Jonah is a very popular story that explains how important it is to stay connected to God and remain obedient to Him (Jonah Chapters 1-3). Let's briefly review the events that happened in the life of Jonah:

> S.I.S. – Use this outline to follow and study the events that happen with Jonah's disobedience.

1. The word of the Lord came to Jonah. (1:1-2)
2. Jonah chose to be disobedient, therefore causing him to become spiritually disconnected from God. (1:3)
3. Disobeying the will of God placed Jonah's life in danger and those around him. (1:4-10)
4. Disobedience automatically separates us from the presence of God. Jonah was thrown overboard and swallowed by a fish, a situation he described as a type of Hell. (1:11-17, 2:1)
5. Jonah realized that his disobedience to God caused him end up in this hellish place, and then he repent and

vowed to obey God. (2:2-9)

6. God forgave Jonah and spoke to the fish containing him, which then vomited him onto dry land where he ended up right where God wanted him to be. (2:10)

7. God spoke to Jonah again and told him to go and do what He commanded him to do.

Through those seven steps, we see the Lord speaking: disobedience, separation from God, consequences, repentance, restoration, and reconnection. Being connected and remaining connected to God means the difference between life and death for you, and perhaps even, someone else. Seems like a lot of pressure. I know. But it is only as difficult as your ability to be obedient. It is important to emphasize this in the case of Jonah: Even after Jonah's disobedience, God still placed him back on the right path at the point of Jonah's sincere repentance. Final thought: How do you keep your soul connected? Repent.

CHAPTER SEVEN:
A CONNECTED SOUL
(WORK SECTION)

How has your life changed from being connected to God through His Spirit living inside you? From the example of a baby and the mother being connected by the umbilical cord, what is being filter in and what is being filter out of you?

_____

_____

_____

_____

_____

_____

_____

_____

_____

_____

_____

How does obedience to God play a part in our connection with Him?

_____

_____

_____

_____
_____
_____
_____
_____
_____
_____

How does love constitute obedience (John 14:15)?

_____
_____
_____
_____
_____
_____
_____
_____
_____
_____

God's will must be fulfill in our lives or we will find it hard to live outside of His will. The Story of Jonah shows this very intricately. Read this story and with the outline in the book, tell some relatable moments you have with this. (Homework)

_____
_____

_____
_____
_____
_____
_____
_____
_____
_____
_____
_____
_____
_____
_____
_____
_____
_____
_____
_____
_____

Staying connected and on target should be the desire of every Christian. Write down somethings that you are going to do in order to keep your commitment to God and stay connected to Him.

_____

Additional Notes

PREPARATION FOR MY SOUL

ONE OF THE GREATEST FEELINGS YOU GET FROM having a targeted soul is the feeling you get from knowing that you are pleasing God with your life. Focusing on reaching heaven should not create a tunnel vision effect. In other words, your focus is pinpointed on heaven, but your heart is postured to reach, teach, and admonish others to make heaven their focus as well. Take into consideration that being focused takes preparation and attention. "Preparation?" you may ask, "What preparation is needed to target my soul?" Well, the first thing you would need to prepare to focus and target your soul is to receive Christ as your Lord and Savior. The problem is that some people think that it stops there and that no other preparation is needed, which is a trage-dy. We are in need of constant and consistent preparation in order to reach our targeted destination. What are these preparations that are needed and why do we need them? In this discussion, I will bring out some points that are very important which pertains to the Christian walk and the targeting of our souls.

"And the very God of peace sanctify you wholly; and I pray God your whole spirit and soul and body be preserved blameless unto the coming of our Lord Jesus Christ" (1 Thessalonians 5:23). Once again—and this cannot be emphasized enough— targeting your soul is a lifestyle and a conscious decision that must be made on a day to day, hour by hour, minute by minute basis. This passage of scripture is preceded by instructions from Paul, which gives the Believer instructions on what to do and what not to do. More importantly, expressed in verses 4-6 is that we are not in darkness, but we are the children of light. I just have one question: Have you ever tried to hit a target in the dark? Yes, that would be quite difficult; spiritually, it is impossible. Do you remember the scripture that talks about the blind leading the blind unless they both fall into a ditch (Mathew 15:14)? Unless we are depending on God to lead and guide us to our souls' destination, let's just say, there is a ditch awaiting us.

Careful preparation requires attention to life's little details, those little things like the small foxes that keep us from staying on course. Walking in the light, being careful to be sober, comforting one another, edifying one another, knowing and loving your leaders in the Lord, warning the unruly, comforting the feeble-minded, supporting the weak, being patient, not rendering evil for evil, following that which is good, rejoicing evermore, praying without ceasing, in everything giving thanks, quenching not the Spirit of God, despising not prophesies, proving all things; holding fast that which is good, and abstaining from all appearance of evil as outlined in 1 Thessalonians 5:11-22, these are the instructions that Paul left the church so that we might not fall into the traps of the enemy and so that we may stay in a place where God can keep and sanctify us both spiritually and physically.

Wow! Did we just say sanctify? A word that is usually used in reference to denominational and church dress codes when, in actuality, it refers to the predestined call of a Believer and the position of a soul that is doing the will of our Father. The word "sanctify" means "to be set aside for a specific use." In the process of sanctification is preparation for used. The God of gods and the King of kings stands as the only One we should serve and be used by. In Leviticus 20:1-8, God told Moses to warn the children of Israel not to serve the god Molech, and those who would serve this god would be put to death. A little history please! Thank you! Molech required the sacrificing of children; therefore, serving this god would not only have killed the parents but also the seed of the children of Israel who would be God's chosen vessels. For these vessels to be used by another god and sacrifice God's precious children would be a slap in God's face. God said He would set His face against the person who serves another god and cut them off from among His people because "He hath given of his seed unto Molech, to defile His sanctuary, and to profane His holy name." So, what was supposed to be set aside for God was now being given to a false god. Imagine the fury and anger this must have caused God to feel, fury to the point of God declaring that if a man knew someone that offered their seed to Molech and did not kill them, He would cut that man and his family off. So, in verses 7 and 8, God told the children of Israel, "Sanctify yourselves therefore, and be ye holy: for I am the Lord your God. And ye shall keep my statutes, and do them: I am the Lord which sanctify you." God is calling for His children to prepare their souls through sanctification first, and then be

Holy.

Whoa! Stop again! Did God just say be holy? Is being holy a part of your soul's preparation to hit its target? Yes, it most definitely is. As a matter of fact, I believe this is one preparation we neglect the most. While we often consider ourselves to be children of God (sanctified), to live the life of holiness unto God is a standard we are usually willing to put aside due to our personal desires. What does it mean to be holy? It simply means to be clean from all sinful acts of the flesh. 1 Peter 1:16 reads: "Because it is written, be ye holy; for I am Holy." Holiness is not a religion, it is a lifestyle, and it is the soul's preparation to meet a holy God. I know you are asking, "Can one be unholy in the presence of a holy God."

There is one thing that you can rest assured when it comes to our God: He will never give us a requirement without making provisions for us to achieve it. While being holy is the requirement, living holy is the goal. Is God expecting us to live a sinless life in order to maintain this standard of holiness? That would be impossible. Instead, God provided us with an antidote for the sin-disease which can cleanse us from sin's stains; and once cleansed, we are then presented holy in the site of God.

David saw himself in a bad position after he committed hideous sins in the eye sight of God, one being putting a man to death and sleeping with that man's wife and having a child with her. After realizing that God was extremely angry with him, David turned back to God and asked for forgiveness in a very interesting way. Sin is referred to as something filthy and dirty, which is the very opposite of holiness. So, what do you do with something that is dirty? Psalm 51:2 says, "Wash me thoroughly from mine iniquity, and cleanse me from my sin." Verse 7 says, "Purge me with hyssop and I shall be clean: wash me, and I shall be whiter than snow." Knowing that sin will occur because that's what we are made of, being cleanse from sin is God's love shown to us.

The natural body that needs to be cleansed from day to day depending on how much dirt you accumulate on your body throughout the day; and the longer you wait to cleanse your physical body, the more evident it will become that you need to cleanse your body. Well, people of God, sin works the same way. We must cleanse daily; more than one time a day, I'm sure. Not having a heart to ask for forgiveness means sin is running through your soul and contaminating your life more and more. It is awesome to know that we have a Heavenly Father who loves us so much that He does not want us to stay in a dirty and sinful state. Do you want to be clean? Do you want to be holy? 1 John 1:9 says, "If we confess our sins, He is faithful and just to forgive us our sins, and to cleanse us from all unrighteousness." That's all there is to it. It seems to me that God has taken most of the hit for our sins. All we have to do is acknowledge our sins and ask God for forgiveness. He is faithful to His Word and His creation. Our Father cleanses us from the dirt of sin. Holiness and righteousness are preparations our souls must take in order to reach our soul's target.

Oh my! Did you say righteousness? Now, why would you want to throw out another word like that, knowing that it would have to be addressed. Righteousness is another preparation our souls must take. It is a state of being that can only be declared by the One who is righteous. Some try to establish their own righteousness and declare themselves to be so, but only God, through His grace and mercy, can declare us to be righteous. It's important to note that you can't measure righteousness by your standards. It's not about what you think is right. "Right" must be judged by God's standards and His holy Word. Psalm 11:7 says, "For the righteous Lord loves righteousness; His countenance doth behold the upright." Now, that is beautiful. Those who are just trying to do right and trying to live holy, God smiles on them as a proud father would his child who is doing well. We serve a righteous God and all His ways are upright. Remember that He expects us to act in an upright manner. One of the reasons for preparing your soul is so that you can have attributes that look like your Father's. 1 John 2:29 says, "If ye know that He is righteous, ye know that every one that doeth righteousness is born of Him." I am a product of my Father if I practice righteousness and prepare my soul through sanctification, holiness and righteousness for what God expects me to be and do in life.

CHAPTER EIGHT:
PREPARATION FOR MY SOUL
(WORK SECTION)

Preparation is needed to target your soul to reach its target. Prior planning prevents poor performance (5 P's). How do we prepare our souls to reach heaven? Give scriptural references to support your comments:

_____

_____

_____

_____

_____

_____

_____

_____

_____

_____

_____

_____

_____

_____

_____

_____

_____

_____

_____

_____

_____

Sanctification, holiness, and righteousness were discussed in detail in this section. These are soul preparations to hit your heavenly target. How have these words been misused? How now do you see them a target for you to reach your soul's target? (Homework)

Sanctification:

_____

_____

_____

_____

_____

_____

_____

_____

_____

_____

_____

_____

_____

_____

_____

_____

_____

_____

_____

_____

_____

Holiness:

_____

_____

_____

_____

_____

_____

_____

_____

_____

_____

_____

_____

_____

_____

_____

_____

_____

_____

_____

_____

Righteuosness:

_____

_____

_____

_____

_____

_____

_____

_____

_____

_____

_____

_____

_____

_____

_____

_____

_____

CHAPTER NINE

SOUL PROTECTION

I PRAY THAT ONE OF THE MAIN THINGS YOU ARE GATHERING from this instructional book is an understanding of how important your soul is. I would like to jump right into this next segment and approach it from two areas:

1. How do you protect your soul?
2. Who is helping you protect your soul?

In section one, we discussed not putting your soul in the hands of the thief: Satan. Your soul is so important that God set up a support system for you so that you wouldn't have to look after your soul all alone. No matter what you say or think, you cannot target your soul alone. We all need someone to help us stay focused, to help us see things a little clearer, or to enlighten us in the Word of God. As pastors, ministers, preachers, bishops, apostles, prophets, evangelists, and all other leaders in the ministry, we have a huge responsibility and we are held accountable for the souls we lead, especially the ones we cause to miss the mark. Hebrews 13:17 gives a wonderful glimpse of the responsibilities of both the "soul's owner" and the soul's "watchman". Let's take a look at both to see their individual responsibilities.

"Obey them that have the rule over you, and submit yourselves: for they watch for your souls, as they that must give account, that they may do it with joy, and not with grief: for that is unprofitable" (Hebrews 13:17). I want to first discuss the responsibilities of the watchman. As stated above, the watchman takes on great responsibility and will have to answer to God for misleading and misdirection any soul that has been placed under his or her care. At the same time, the writer also encourages the soul's owner not to make protecting their soul a daunting task as that would not be good for them when the watchman goes to give their report to God. As leaders, it would give us great joy to be able to tell God that the sheep He placed in our care are the best the pasture has to offer. As it is unprofitable to have to give a bad report, it is be profitable to be able to give a good report. Just remember this though: All of this comes through obedience to your leaders.

God gives very clear understanding about the importance of a watchman in Ezekiel 33:1-7. There, He set Ezekiel to be a watchman over the children of Israel. Let's look at these verses and bring to light how the watchman is a protector over the souls of men:

Verses 1 & 2—God tells Ezekiel that the people must first realize the need for a watchman. If we don't accept the watchman God sent us we won't heed their warnings which are given to them from God. The watchman's position has been tainted by those who have been untrustworthy and without integrity; therefore, the calling has been under much scrutiny. That still does not nullify the need for a watchman, nor does it provide us with an excuse for being misdirected. The point is you need to know your watchmen; furthermore, you need to try them by the Holy Spirit because their words and their life will affect those they watch over.

Verse 3—This verse is the beginning of the watchman's responsibility and defines two distinct characteristics the watchman must have:

1. He/she must be attentive and sensitive to the urgency and importance of his/her position. God told Ezekiel that the watchman has to see the danger coming upon the land and then take action. As a protector of the souls, God allows us to see the enemy coming in any and all forms he may take. So many times God will allow a watchman to see things that the enemy has blinded other individuals from seeing. This is definitely one reason why it's important to know who your watchman is and to know that he/she truly hears from God.
2. After seeing danger approaching on the horizon, the watchman must react by blowing the trumpet to warn others. To blow the trumpet at the sight of danger is to actually save the lives (souls) of those who would hear and listen to the warning being put out. The trumpet is the voice of the men and woman of God; it should be sounded when the enemy is seen trying to trap the souls of God's people and get them off target.

Verse 4 & 5—It's one thing to blow a trumpet and warning of impending danger, but it's another thing for the warning to be received and acted on. Don't neglect the job and responsibility of the watchman—he/she is not the boy who cried wolf. The watchman really does see what he/she sees and hear what he/she hears. God is serious about our souls; therefore, when He tells the watchman to warn His people about things that are going on in their lives or something coming down the line, it is important to take heed. This verse speaks of the person who does not listen to the warning(s) of the watchman and decides to take matters completely their own hands with no regard for the Word of the Lord. This is why in the house of God so many souls fall into the hands of the enemy. So many times warnings go out and the trumpet is blown, and yet, men still walk away as if nothing was said or heard by them. In this case, the watchman did what was required of him/her, and therefore, the blood or loss of the soul of the one who refused to listen is that individual's fault.

Verse 6—The other side of this would be the watchman not doing what he/she is supposed to do by failing to warn those he/she has been placed over—they've chosen not to blow the horn when they saw danger coming. This particular warning from God to the watchman should be taken with the utmost concern. Having lives in your hands and not doing all that it takes to save those souls from death and destruction is a failure that God will not tolerate. If you have been set up as a watchman by God, that means He has chosen you and communicates to you important information concerning His people. To keep your mouth closed when God says speak up and warn others is to literally allow the enemy to come in and do what he wants to do, which is to kill, steal, and destroy. What's important is that the watchmen avoids getting caught up and distracted with other things and fails to do what they have been commissioned by God to do. We have watchmen in this present time who have been inundated with messages of wealth and prosperity which has resulted in them misleading others' souls. Some watchmen have become so immersed in their own inspiring and enticing preaching that even after all of their "celebrating" and "tuning" lives are still not being changed—there is no crying out for salvation from the souls sitting in the pews. So, when the watchman fails to blow the horn, and the lives (souls) are snatched away by sin and iniquity, God said the blood of those lost souls will rest on the hands of their particular watchmen.

Verse 7—Make sure that your soul is so important to you that you find a watchman who will tell you what God says regardless of whether or not it hurts your feelings or even makes you angry. The important thing is that your life is saved. God told Ezekiel in the latter part of verse seven, "…therefore thou shalt hear the word at my mouth, and warn them from me." The connection between God and His watchman demonstrates the love God has for His creation, God gives words of warning to His watchmen to give to His people so that He can protect them. The souls' proprietors are responsible for picking the right watchmen for their souls. When choosing their watchmen, they must select someone who will fully preach and teach the truth of God and nothing but the truth, not one who will them what they want to hear. In 2 Timothy 4:2-4, Paul warned Timothy to be a good watchman, "For the time will come when they will not endure sound doctrine; but after their own lusts shall they heap to themselves teachers, having itching ears; and they shall turn away their ears from the truth, and shall be turned unto fables." This is true today because it seems as if people only want to hear what makes them feel good; they're being told things by watchmen that

God never told them to say. But the things that will lead them into a true relationship with God and will help them aim their souls at the target of eternity in heaven, let's just say that trumpet isn't being blown.

S.I.S. – Please Consider: Always remember that it's your soul that is at stake. If you realize that the watchman over your soul is not leading you towards eternity in heaven but they're lying to you by telling you that God will accept you any way despite your lifestyle and sinful actions, and that holiness is not necessary, then it is time for you to find a new watchman.

CHAPTER NINE:
SOUL PROTECTION
(WORK SECTION)

Soul protection is important and must be taken very seriously for more than one reason. Let's discuss Satan's plans for your soul. Discuss some of the plots that you have seen the devil try to carry out in your life and describe how God protected you from them:

_____

_____

_____

_____

_____

_____

_____

_____

_____

_____

_____

_____

_____

_____

_____

_____

_____

_____

_____

_____

There are those who God has sanctioned to protect the souls of others; they are referred to as "Watchmen". What are the duties of a watchman according to Scripture (Old and New Testament)? (Homework)

_____

_____

_____

_____

_____

_____

_____

_____

_____

_____

_____

_____

_____

Do you personally feel you need a watchman in your life to cover your soul? Why or why not?

_____

_____
_____
_____
_____
_____
_____
_____
_____
_____
_____

What type of soul-protector (watchman) are you looking for? What are you not looking for?

_____
_____
_____
_____
_____
_____
_____
_____
_____

Additional Notes

_____

SECTION THREE
FOCUS ON MY SOUL

CHAPTER TEN

WHAT DISTRACTIONS

THERE IS ONE THING THAT IS CERTAIN TO COME TO A person who is focused on achieving a goal or reaching a destination: distractions. Unfortunately, it is inevitable that anytime you set your sights on something and choose to pursue a dream, vision, lifetime or eternal goal, something is going to happen to try to deter you from reaching that goal. Yes, this also applies to your soul's target. Not only will distractions come, but the more you press forward, the more they will keep coming.

I am reminded of an account in the Bible where Peter saw Jesus walking on the sea. Wanting to partake in that experience, Peter asked Jesus to allow him to join Him on the water. I can imagine that this was a wonderful experience for Peter. As long as he stayed focused and kept his eyes on the target, which was Jesus, Peter was fine. What is ironic about this story—and seems to likewise be in our lives—is that the worst thing that could have happened did happen, which caused Peter to be distracted. The main purpose for distractions is to cause you to lose focus. Trust me, distractions serve no other purpose. In Peter's case, how convenient was it that a storm would rumble through as soon as he set his sights on Jesus? It was bold enough to begin with that Peter would dare ask to walk on water, but to be faced with the distracting waves of the sea and possible death, that was too much for Peter to handle. Yes, the perfectly timed distraction got the best of him. He lost sight of the target and started to sink. This is a true testament to not staying focused on the target and allowing distractions to get you off course. Thank God for salvation. Even when we lose focus, God will come and grab our hands and bring us back up.

It's not the distractions that are the problem; we already know that they are coming. The problem is when we don't see the distractions for what they are, and we lose sight of what they are here to accomplish. Don't be deceived. Distractions are strategically placed in our lives to throw us off target. They wouldn't be distractions if they couldn't get our attention. Sometimes it seems like just as soon as you feel as if you have finally gotten focused, all of a sudden something hits you like a flood. Just as Peter was focusing on getting to Jesus, then came the winds. Believe me when I tell you, there is nothing subtle about a distraction: it can be a big wind or a small wind, an all-out stare-down or just a wink, a long conversation or just a comment. In any case, it will always be an aggressive act to gain our attention. These distractions can come in all shapes and sizes; they can be friends, family, and foes. We must be determined not to let anything or anyone get us off target.

The worst way to react to a distraction is to entertain and tolerate it. Nothing good can come out of you permitting something or someone that you know is a distraction to hang around and continue to eat away at you like a canker worm. Let's visit a man who was given a purpose by God from his birth and eventually become a judge over the children of Israel: Samson.

Samson was a man of war who would use his supernatural strength which was given to him by God to avenge and bring security to the people of God. As long as he stayed focus and didn't reveal to anyone the source of his strength, he would be a great warrior in the army of God. Among his many vices and his riddling personality, there was one problem Samson had that would eventually be a distraction in his life leading to his downfall: Samson's love for women. The enemy does not have to be a rocket scientist to figure out your weaknesses, and he knows how to use them as a weapon against you. Sooner or later, if you prove yourself to be vulnerable, you will succumb to that weakness.

Let's continue on with the story: Samson met a woman named Delilah and, of course, with his problematic nature, he found it difficult to resist her and ended up falling in love with her. No doubt, Delilah had some regard for Samson but was given an offer she could not refuse. So she became a distraction to Samson and brought him down. Note: Remember Peter? If the distraction causes you to lose sight of your target, you will go down.

Judges 16:5-17 explains how Samson's distraction was put in place and reveals the events that transpired which led to his great fall. There are a few things in this passage that reveals how destructive it is to entertain something you know is there to bring you down. Although Samson used Delilah to defeat many Philistines, the game went on too long and Delilah ended up getting what she was looking for. Let's look at verse 16: it reads, "And it came to pass when she pressed him daily with her words, and urged him, so that his soul was vexed unto death." Notice here that the desperate attempts of the distraction prevailed: Samson's soul began to get so overwhelmed with worry over Delilah. He would rather have died than have her ask him once more about the source of his strength. It's amazing that he could withstand all the attacks of the Philistines but he couldn't handle the plotting of one manipulative woman. He decided to play and keep his distraction around him.

The demise of Samson was a loss for the targeted and a win for the distraction. Because he lost to his distraction, he ended up enduring many afflictions and persecutions including having his eyes put out as a form of punishment. But the worst punishment he experienced was knowing that he had been distracted, manipulated, and stripped of the presence of the Lord (vs. 20). There are so many people, preachers, ministers, and evangelists who have been distracted by the world and by things that are not of God causing the Spirit of God to leave them. Even still, there is restoration after distraction.

Samson suffered great loss at the hands of his distraction, but he asked God for forgiveness and God avenged him especially for the torture he endured and the putting out of his eyes. God moved on Samson one last time and gave him the strength to kill over three thousand Philistines who were there to make a mockery of him; this included all of the Philistine lords—they all died at the hands of Samson, which he requested of God. The Bible declares that Samson, upon his death, killed more Philistines than he did during his entire life. Once again, there is hope after being distracted. Just because a distraction cost Samson his life, it doesn't have to cost you yours. God can still use you if you choose to ask God for forgiveness and get back on target. That's the great thing about God: He covers us with love, and takes even our mistakes and shortcomings and uses them in His overall plan for our lives. Because of God's mercy and grace, we have an opportunity to make peace with God.

Soul distractions come in many different forms and from many different people—sometimes from the people who are closest to you. Have you ever been discouraged, put down, let down, cast down, or felt someone trying to pull you in a direction that you knew was ungodly or in a direction you knew God was not taking you? So many distractions. Even God addressed certain distractions in Deuteronomy. God further warned His children that any excuse for them losing their focus was acceptable. "If thy brother, the son of thy mother, or thy son, or thy daughter, or the wife of thy bosom, or thy friend, which is as thine own soul, entice thee secretly, saying; Let us go and serve other gods, which thou hast not known, thou, nor thy fathers; Thou shall not consent unto, him, nor hearken unto him; neither shall thine eye pity him, neither shalt thou spare, neither shalt thou conceal him: But thou shalt surely kill him. Thine hand shall be first upon him to put him to death, and afterward the hand of all the people" (Deuteronomy 13:6, 8, 9). It really does not get any clearer than that. God shows no pity for those who will distract His people and get them off their soul target.

Please keep in mind that anything can become a "god" if it is placed before or above the one true and living God. Plainly stated, anything that can cause you to lose sight of your target has the potential to be something you will eventually worship. Be careful to avoid allowing anyone to entice you to serve another god; also, don't lose sight of your commitment to serve God and Him alone. Joshua chimed in on not being distracted in Joshua 24:15 where he boldly declared, "And if seem evil unto you to serve the

129

Lord, choose you this day whom ye will serve: whether the gods which your fathers served that were on the other side of the flood, or the gods of the Amorites, in whose land ye dwell: but as for me and my house, we will serve the Lord." I wonder if there are any targeted and focused children of God who will stand and declare these words: 'I don't care about the past, the present, what others do or don't do whether they be family, friends, or loved ones; I will serve the Lord and not allow any distractions to move me from my commitment to God.'

There is one last area of distraction that I would like to address. Believe it or not, distractions don't always come from outside sources. As matter of fact, the biggest and most influential distraction comes from within ourselves. It is ironic when you think about it—the fact that we often keep ourselves from staying on target. I also realize that these distractions can be very enticing and hard resist because they are fleshly derived and sinfully motivated and are connected to feelings of pleasure and temporary satisfaction. 1 Peter 2:11 says, "Dearly beloved, I beseech you as strangers and pilgrims, abstain from fleshly lusts, which war against the soul". These desires (lusts) that are not of God are the ones used by Satan to place your soul in a tug of war battle. The struggle against your flesh is more difficult than any other struggle when it comes to staying on target. In this struggle, your soul is constantly fighting against your flesh. Peter was addressing those he called strangers and pilgrims—those who are in the body of Christ. Yes, we are not citizens of this world; we have been reborn into the Kingdom of God. With such a rebirth, our souls are connected to God's Kingdom although our flesh desires the things of this world. So, while our souls are aimed at the target of heaven, our flesh desires sin. The Apostle Peter admonished those who are "Kingdom Citizens" and "World Pilgrims" to stay away from the things that will distract us from our journey back home.

Another distraction is the "me, myself, and I" mentality that is cultivated from selfish desires. In other words, many people claim, "I have to do what makes me happy. I just want to enjoy my life." While there is nothing wrong with enjoying life, there is a problem when we seek to enjoy sinful and worldly things. You are not fooling anyone. When this self-centered mentality overtakes us, most likely our actions will not resemble Godly character and activities. The world is the biggest distraction for the flesh; and if not brought under subjection, we will find ourselves chasing after the lusts of the flesh. We must recognize the distraction of the world and adhere to the writings of Paul in 2 Corinthians 6:17-18 where he admonishes us saying, "Wherefore come out from among them, and be ye separate, says the Lord, and touch not the unclean thing; and I will receive you, and will be a Father unto you, and ye shall be my sons and daughters, says the Lord Almighty." The soul is free and liberated only when we can keep the contaminates of worldly lusts away from it. Target your soul to be free and remain free, and don't allow internal distractions to get you off course.

CHAPTER TEN:
WHAT DISTRACTIONS
(WORK SECTION)

What dreams and visions have you been deterred from? What was the distraction?

_____
_____
_____
_____
_____
_____
_____

Are you back on track? What did you do to get back on track?

_____
_____
_____
_____
_____
_____
_____
_____
_____
_____
_____

What does a convenient storm mean to you (mostly incon-venient)?

_____

_____

_____

_____

_____

_____

_____

_____

_____

_____

_____

_____

_____

Concerning Samson, why do you think he tolerated Delilah for so long?

_____

_____

_____

_____

_____

_____

Distractions can come from so many different areas and even those closest to you. Have you ever had to choose between following a close loved one (husband, wife, child, etc.) or doing the will of God? Which did you choose and how hard was it to make that decision?

_____

_____

_____

_____

_____

_____

_____

_____

_____

_____

_____

_____

_____

Sometimes we can be our own biggest distraction. What are some distractions we bring against ourselve? What are some of the self-inflicted distractions you face that keeps you off target? (Homework)

_____

_____

_____

_____

_____

_____

_____

_____

Additional Notes

_____

_____

_____

_____

_____

_____

_____

_____

_____

_____

_____

_____

_____

_____

_____

_____

CHAPTER ELEVEN

WHERE DID I LOSE TRACK?

Piggybacking off of the distractions we discussed in our previous chapter, we need to expound further on the issue of where and how we get off track. It is important to point out the cause of our falls. It's important to confess your faults and realizing that you have weaknesses. A person must take an assessment of his/her life and address the things that might distract him/her. They must look hard and take note of the fact that every time "this" particular thing happens or "that" particular person comes around, or whenever they arrive to "that" job or when "that" person looks at them, or even when they focus only on themselves they tend to stumble and fall. We must not lose hope simply because we've lost our way. God is the master of putting His people back on the right path.

Do you remember when our good friend the Apostle Peter made the decision to get out of the boat and walk on water to go to Jesus? After Peter began to sink, Jesus reached out His hand to catch him and pull him up. Jesus asked Peter a very important question; He asked Peter, "O thou of little faith, wherefore did thou doubt?" Note that this question came to Peter after he was actually walking on water but allowed the waves, thunder, and lightning to take his eyes off of Jesus. So, if Peter was doing so well, what happened? Where did he lose track? Jesus called it "doubt". Doubt played a major role in Peter's distraction. I wondered why Jesus said doubt rather than fear? Consider this: Peter looked at the elements before he began to sink; but if you remember, the winds and waves of the sea were already roaring before Peter got out of the ship. When Peter first saw Jesus, he believed he would be alright if he was out there with the Savior; therefore, fear was not the contributing factor in this scenario. The major factor was Peter's uncertainty as to how far his faith would take him.

So many times we will take a leap of faith, jump out the boat and put our souls on target; but then, after a while, after experiencing troubled waters, we will start to lose focus and think that we are much safer back in the ship. We then start to doubt that God called us out of the boat and onto the water. Perhaps it's because when Jesus says "come" we expect the winds to stop blowing and the rain to stop falling. But Jesus never told us that we would not have to face any hard times on the journey towards our targets; He only promised that He would be with us. On our journeys, Jesus is asking us the same question He asked Peter: When did you lose focus and get off track? When did you stop trusting that God is on the water with you?

The doubt factor is definitely an issue when comes to staying on target. Why aim for a target but doubt that you will actually hit it? If doubt is anywhere in the scope of you hitting your soul's target, then most likely you will miss it.

So many times we are faced with the challenges of life and wonder how we will make it through. But though your faith may get challenged, it should never get lost. In order for us to walk on the waters of life, we must stay focused on Jesus and believe that He will keep us in every situation.

Keeping your soul on target is like following a good GPS on your way to a certain destination. There is nothing like looking at the screen or hearing the voice of the GPS system telling you where to go. You hit every landmark, make every turn, and finally make it to your destination in the amount of time given to you. These systems have become so advanced that they can tell you where the traffic is and if there's a car on the side of the road, and they can predict any delays that are involved in your journey. On the other hand, there have been times when I trusted a GPS to get me to a destination, but it took me where I didn't desire to go which in turn put me in somewhat of a dilemma since I was totally dependent upon the GPS. And now that I'm not where I want to be, I immediately begin to feel lost. At what point did I lose my way? Where did I make the wrong turn? Believe it or not, it is quite easy to lose your way and get off target even when you're confident that you are going in the right direction.

> S.I.S. – The lost factor is overwhelming. Explain how this has effected your faith.

This entire book is about teaching you what to do and what not to do in order to keep your soul on target. Sometimes we follow voices that we trust, and yet, those voices are not of God; and if we continue to follow these voices, before you know it, spiritually you will end up somewhere you didn't intend to be without having a clue as to how you got there. But I am so grateful for God's Provisional System (GPS), which can bring us out of any mess, out of any situation, and put us back on track when we call on the Lord's name. God's system is wonderful! He will let us know through His Spirit where the enemy is, how he is trying to trick and detour us, where the fiery darts are, and where the stumbling blocks the enemy has set up to get our souls off target are. That's a good place to lift your hands and tell God thank you for saving your life and keeping you on target. Finally, God's Provisional System is guaranteed to take you to your destination. If heaven is your destination, who better to lead you there than the Spirit of the living God? Amen!

CHAPTER ELEVEN:
WHERE DID I LOSE TRACK?
(WORK SECTION)

One of the purposes of this book is to help you look deep down into your soul and discover the things that will prevent you from aiming for and reaching heaven (taking an assessment spiritually). What's planted deep in your soul (consciousness) that you feel is keeping you off target and unfocused? (Note: this is a little different from a distraction, but could be the result of a distraction.)

_____

_____

_____

_____

_____

_____

_____

_____

_____

_____

_____

_____

_____

_____

_____

_____

_____

_____

_____

_____

_____

_____

Does the soul issue present a struggle in you as it pertains to your spiritual life? If so, what type of struggle is it and what do you do to cope with the struggle?

_____

_____

_____

_____

_____

_____

_____

_____

_____

_____

_____

_____

_____

_____

_____

_____

The worst part about losing track is the fact that we take our eyes off of Christ. According to our study of Mathew 14:22-33, can you see the similarities between what took place in the case with Peter and what is taking place in your life? If so, elaborate on those similarities below: (Homework)

Peter seeing Jesus on the water:

_____

_____

_____

_____

_____

_____

_____

_____

Peter asking Jesus to bid him to come (take into account the winds and waves that were blowing):

_____

_____

_____

_____

_____

_____

_____

Jesus tells Peter to come and he gets out the boat:

_____

_____

_____

_____

_____

_____

_____

Peter is walking on the water, going towards Jesus:

_____

_____

_____

_____

_____

_____

_____

Peter is distracted by a boisterous winds:

_____

_____

_____

_____

_____

_____

Peter begins to sink and cry out for help:

_____

_____

_____

_____

_____

_____

_____

Jesus saves Peter's life and asks him, "Wherein did he doubt":

_____

_____

_____

_____

_____

_____

_____

This section brings in the "doubt factor" as it pertains to losing focus and losing ground. Has doubt ever played a factor in your 'walking on water experience'?

_____

_____

_____

_____

_____

_____

_____

_____

_____

_____

_____

_____

_____

_____

To be on track and then suddenly fall off track is a feeling unlike any other. Explain in your own words how you felt when you first discovered that you had lost track of where you were going in Christ:

_____

_____

_____

_____

_____

_____

_____

_____

_____

_____

_____

CHAPTER TWELVE

How Do I Get Back Focused?

"**B**UT WHEN HE SAW THE WIND BOISTEROUS HE WAS afraid; and beginning to sink, he cried, 'Lord, save me'" (Matthew 14:30). The key words here are "Lord, save me." This is a desperate cry from someone who feels their life is in serious danger. A soul that is not targeted to reach heaven is in much worse shape than Peter was in; even still, Jesus is still the answer; He still saves to the upmost. Jesus saves us and let us know that we are not too far gone for Him to reach out His loving hand and grab us and bring us back up.

Once you have realized that you have been distracted and you know where the distraction is coming from, then the next step is to do what it takes to regain focus, get back on track, and prepare to keep moving. By now, you should really be taking your soul very seriously and not be willing to lose it at any cost, and be ready to hit its eternal mark. It's not about actually losing focus; it's really about how fast you can recover and get back focused on heaven.

There is a very familiar story in the Bible, a parable if you will, found in Luke 15:12-24. There, Jesus tells a story about a man who had two sons. One of the sons became interested in life outside of the safety of his father and asked his father to give him of his portion of goods that he was entitled to. At the son's request, the father did just that and gave him his inheritance, and then that son took off and traveled to a faraway land. He began to live the fast life and waste all of his inheritance, not worrying about how he would later have to live and take care of himself. Jesus continued and said that when the young man had spent all that he had, a great famine arose in the land and the young man didn't have anything to sustain himself; he found that he was now in great need. The young man met up with a citizen of the country who employed him to feed the swine. The young man began to be in such great need that he started to eat the husks that were supposed to be for the pigs. No one gave him anything. But Jesus provided a key lesson in this parable that should be an answer for all of us who have been distracted and have lost our way for one reason or another. Verse 17 says, "And when he came to himself…" I must pause right there and point out that if you are ever going to get focused, you must come to yourself and recognize that you are in a place that you don't need to be and have done some things you shouldn't have done. So many of us, just like this son, think that we are ready to take life into our own hands and we leave the safety of the loving God who is taking care of us and meeting every one of our needs. I can guarantee you this: God has a way of making you see that you need Him and that you are His child, and that leaving Him should never be an option for your life.

Now back to the story: The young man had an

epiphany and realized that in his father's house there was plenty of food and supplies even for the servants, and he began to wonder why was he eating with pigs and suffering to the point of starvation needlessly. He then laid down his pride and made the right choice to go back to his father and ask for forgiveness. To everyone that will hear and read the words of this book, please remember that we have a Heavenly Father who forgives and is always waiting for us to return when we stray, get distracted, and lose focus. Just cry out to God and ask for His forgiveness. He loves you and will bring you back to Him and place your soul back on track to hit your eternal target.

Okay, let's finish the story. The young man already had his repentance speech prepared for when he saw his father, but once he was approaching his father's house, the father saw him coming from far off and ran to his son and grabbed him and kissed him, glad that his son had come back home. The father put on a great feast, adorned his son with a ring of gold, and celebrated the return of his son. The final thought I want to bring out of this story is that God is waiting for us to return to to Him. There is nothing that He loves more than a soul that is aimed at heaven. For Believers, we can rest assured that we will be received by our Heavenly Father with loving, open arms some day, and we will hear Him say, "Welcome home my child!"

David talked in the 23rd Psalm about God's love and grace concerning the souls of His people. He wrote, "He restores my soul: He leads me in the path of righteousness for His name sake." My, oh my. How this one verse speaks volumes as to how much God desires for us to stay on target. When we have become depleted, distracted, disoriented, displeased, and discouraged, we are restored through our Father's love and care. How great is our God in all the earth!

149

Oh, how He loves us so unconditionally; so much so that He sees our frail and fallen state and give us an opportunity through grace to accept the sacrifice of His Son. That breath (His Spirit) that we lost in the Garden of Eden can now be restored to us. It is also that same Spirit who leads and guides us in the path that will please the Father and who keeps our souls on track so that we will someday meet the Father in heaven.

I want to suggest that if you feel as if you have gotten off track and know that the distractions of life and sin have overtaken you, just recommit yourself to Christ and allow God to help you get things back in order. I submit to you this truth: getting focused for some could take a process. No, I'm not giving you an excuse to sin, but I am saying that salvation and staying fixed upon your target is an everyday life journey. So, don't sweat it when you fall or start to sink; at least you had the will to step out of the boat and onto the water.

1 Peter 4:19 says, "Wherefore, let them that suffer according to the will of God commit the keeping of their souls to Him in well doing, as unto a faithful Creator." Oh, yes. Peter, I hear you talking to me now. I realize that choosing God sometimes means you will have to suffer. As a matter of fact, verse 12 of that same chapter says, "Beloved, think it not strange concerning the fiery trial which is to try you, though some strange thing happened unto you." There is nothing like a fiery trial that will come and try to take you off track and keep you from having victory in your life. But believe it or not, those fiery trials serve two purposes: the first is to let you know that you are on target because you are suffering for the name sake of Christ, and the second is to keep you on target. Truth be told, fiery darts will take you out if you don't depend on Jesus and His salvation. Pe-

ter says to commit your soul into the hands of to God and continue in well doing, and when you are doing the best you can to stay on target, God will, in return, take care of you just as He promised. God is a faithful Creator and will definitely take care of His own.

There are three last things I want to talk about when it comes to getting back focused and getting in position to reach your soul's target. If you ever find yourself off target, try these three things:

1. Adjust your Site- Desire the Word of God
2. Focus on the Target- Hear the Word of God
3. Commit to the Target- Be obedient to the Word of God

Adjust your Site. Have you ever had to adjust the lens of a camera, a scope, or a projector? The reason for making that adjustment is because something that you were looking at was blurred and poorly focused. In order for you to get a clear look at what you are focusing in upon, you may have to take time to do some twists and turns of the lens. While targeting your soul we must endeavor to take that same approach albeit spiritually. Sometimes we lose focus on God's Kingdom—our spiritual attention is diverted to worldly things or we just simply get discouraged. At that time, what we need to focus on is blurred and obscured. But not to worry. All we really need are some spiritual eye drops—something to clear up our spiritual vision and help us to see our eternal target again. There is nothing better than God's Word that can set us back on track and get us refocused, but there must be a desire in your heart to first see where you are, how you got off track, and that you NEED to do to get back on track. Without a desire for the sincere milk of Christ's Word and the wisdom to seek His righteousness, we are like cameras with the lens cover still on—unable to focus because we have blinders over our eyes. The desire for God's Word creates a hunger and thirst for His righteousness inside of us which causes us to intensely seek to stay on target.

Focus on the Target. Once you have adjusted your sight to hit the right target, you must stay focused on that target. Heaven is our goal, and it is accessible to all those who have received Christ as their Savior. But please don't think that hitting the heavenly target is going to be a cake walk. We have an adversary who will stop at nothing to keep us from making heaven our home. What's going to keep you focused? What's going to keep your mind from wavering, your heart from hurting, and your soul from the dark?

Well, the same way you adjusted a lens when working a camera is the same way you stay focused on the target you want to hit. You have to desire, indulge, and let God's Word take root in your heart. Psalm 119:11 expresses the steadfastness we need in order to stay on target. It says, "Thy word have I hid in mine heart, that I might not sin against thee." Beautifully put! It should be an anthem for every born again Believer. Can you feel the heart of David? Tired of getting off track; no longer wanting to lose his soul's target. He made a conscious decision to take God's Word—His commandment and statutes—to heart. Remember when we talked about how closely connected the heart and the soul are at the beginning of this book, and how the heart is the very beat of the soul? Well, purposed in your heart that you are determined to reach your goal and no devil in hell will throw you off your target.

Understand also that the Word of God comes in different forms. You can get it from the book (Bible), from a preacher who is targeted, from a song of worship and praise, and even a word of prophecy or encouragement; however, when the Word comes, let it edify your soul and take root in your heart because God's ultimate intention in sending His Word is not for His Word to return to Him void, but for His creation to bring it back to Him through obedience.

Commit to the Target. "Ye that love the Lord, hate evil: He preserves the souls of His saints; He delivers them out of the hand of the wicked" (Psalm 97:10). "Jesus said unto him, thou shalt love the Lord thy God with all thy heart, and with all thy soul, and with all thy mind" (Mathew 22:37). The 97th Psalm suggests that God preserves and delivers those that love Him and hate evil. Jesus announced to the Sadducees that to love God is the greatest commandment in the Bible. The only way to stay on target is to commit to the target. Yes, I know heaven is your goal, but if you are not looking to be in the presence of God forever and you only want to get to heaven for free milk and honey, then your desires are too shallow. You have to be committed to seeing your Lord and Savior one day, and loving Him will definitely get you to Him. It goes hand in hand. Jesus said, "If you love me, keep my commandments"(John 14:15). If you keep His commandments you will not sin against Him, and you will also make sure all distractions are put away; therefore, love, being the greatest affection of all, will lead you straight to your target.

Committing to your target takes love (all thy heart), passion (all thy soul), and concentration (all thy mind). Where have we seen this formula before? In our Savior, Jesus Christ. Let's take just a minute to explore a little deeper the intense components of these words as it pertains to the positioning of our souls to hit the mark of eternity:

1. Love—Nothing conquers love, but love conquers all. The love that Jesus referred to is supreme in nature even above that of a mother's, father's, sister's, brother's, child's, friend's, etc.; it's a love for the Creator, the Giver of Life, who is our Heavenly Father, a love that was demonstrated by God who loved the world so much that He gave His only Son. So, the act of love that God expects of us in return is the giving of our lives to Him. A life for a life; a heart for a heart.

2. Passion—The definition of passion is "to be so attached that you can feel everything that affects another emotionally; to include hurt, pain, joy and more." This is why Jesus requires of us to love God with all of our soul. Jesus bore our hurts and pain. Jesus felt what we feel. Jesus was often moved with compassion and felt the deposition of men's hearts. He intertwined His soul with our souls so that His love for us would be shown through His relationship with us. Again, as pertaining to David and Jonathan, this type of love and passion which comes from the soul for another will cause one to give something, and in Jesus' case, give all. We fail to realize that this is one of the reasons Jesus came. He wanted to feel our souls' emotional state, and then return to the Father, sit at His right side, and explain to Him exactly how we feel. Wow! He is our advocate! Committing your soul to a target means being passionate about achieving your goal(s). Have you ever been passionate about accomplishing something in life? What would you give to make sure you achieve it? Why aren't we more passionate about our souls? What is your soul more passionate about than seeing its Creator? Ponder those questions for a while. Consider these questions and then answer

them after examining how much of you you are surrendering to God and whether or not your soul is on track to hit your eternal target.

3. Will—The ability of the mind to concentrate and achieve is one of the most powerful elements we have. It is within the mind that the power of will and choice is manufactured and pushed into manifestation. The mind gives strength to the body to perform what it has decided to do. In an effort to stay focused upon the mission and task at hand, Jesus, in the Garden of Gethsemane, looked at the suffering He was sent to undergo but began to search for another solution; but understanding how important His task was, He "willed" Himself into a state of submission to the will of the Father. Jesus, being all God and all man, put His fleshly will under subjection to the will of His spirit in order to fulfill the will of His Father. Just like the word "purpose", the word "will" has dual meaning, and both definitions are similar to the definitions of the word "purpose".

I pointed out earlier in this book that God requires our hearts and souls to become aligned when giving of one's all to Him. So, why would Jesus also include the mind? God would have to understand the minds of men in order to require that the mind come into alignment with His will and purpose. With His Son coming to dwell among men in the flesh on earth, God would be able to relate to us on our level. Jesus had to master bringing His mind into subjection to the Father's will in order to show us that it can be done with the help of the Father. Paul, in Philippians 2:5-8, said, "Let this mind be in you, which was also in Christ Jesus; Who, being in the form of God, thought it not robbery to be equal with God; But made Himself of no reputation, and took upon Him the form of a servant, and was made in the likeness of men; And being found in fashion as a man, He humbled Himself, and became obedient unto death, even the death of the cross."

One of the greatest actions the mind can take (and I believe this is why Jesus incorporated the mind into the equation with the heart and soul) is to humble itself unto obedience to God. Clearly, obedience is the fulfillment of one's mission and purpose. Jesus was committed to His purpose, and the Bible says we should have that same mind in us. Even love is embodied within obedience. Jesus told His disciples, "If you love me, keep my commandments."

Aligning the heart, soul, and mind in order to reach your soul's target will guarantee a successful journey. I realize that sometimes the heart gets faint, the soul gets weary, and the mind seems unstable; but our loving Father will bring us back into focus if our intentions are to live for Him and to one day see Him in peace.

CHAPTER TWELVE:
HOW DO I GET
BACK FOCUSED?
(WORK SECTION)

After realizing that you got off track, did you find getting back on track easy or hard to do? Tell why:

_____

_____

_____

_____

_____

_____

_____

_____

_____

Concerning the need for self-denial in order to get back on track, it may require some suffering. How important should getting back focused and on target spiritually be to you and what are you willing to suffer for it?

_____

_____

_____

_____

_____

_____

_____

_____

_____

_____

_____

_____

_____

_____

_____

Everyday spent off track is a day spent not focusing on Christ. How do you think Christ feels about not having our devotion, and what do you feel His response is or should be to our doubt?

_____

_____

_____

_____

_____

_____

_____

Three solutions were given in the book to assist you in getting back focused. How do you see yourself practicing these points? (Homework)

Adjust your site:

_____

_____

_____

_____

_____

_____

_____

_____

_____

Focus on the target:

_____

_____

_____

_____

_____

_____

_____

_____

_____

Commit to the target:

_____

_____

_____

_____

_____

_____

_____

_____

_____

We must always use Jesus as our example in all things as we are striving to be Christ-like. How does Jesus' walk relate to the 3 points just mentioned above?

_____

_____

_____

_____

_____

_____

_____

_____

_____

_____

_____

_____

_____

_____

_____

_____

_____

_____

_____

_____

_____

_____

In the commitment section, three intricate areas are mentioned: they are love, passion, and will. Please expound on what they mean to you and how these areas have helped you to get focused and stay focused: (Homework)

Love (conquers all):

_____

_____

_____

_____

_____

_____

_____

_____

_____

_____

Passion (soul connection):

_____

_____

_____

_____

_____

_____

_____

Will (the decision):

_____

_____

_____

_____

_____

_____

_____

_____

_____

CHAPTER THIRTEEN

AM I ON TARGET FOR WHERE I WANT TO BE IN ETERNITY?

WE HAVE REACHED THE FINAL SECTION OF THIS BOOK, and I pray that by now you have made a conscious decision as to where you are going to direct your soul to spend eternity. And not only that, but I pray you also understand that this is a life long journey and that we will have to endure a lot in order to reach our destination. I find joy in knowing that Jesus promised to never leave nor forsake us. We don't have to travel alone. God is there. By His Spirit God leads and guides us to our heavenly eternal destination. It is equally important to mention that a soul that is not aimed at the Kingdom of God but is led by sin into selfish acts of the flesh is destined to reach hell.

By all means, understand that there is no place in between heaven and hell in the afterlife, no waiting grounds, and no holding place for the soul to make a decision. All decisions regarding your soul's eternal home must be made before the breath leaves your body. Sometimes we live our lives as if we are going to live forever, forgetting that we will one day have to leave this earth. But one day we will have to give an account before God for everything we've done in our bodies. And yes, sinner, that includes you! So, unless a decision is made to get on target, you have made your choice to inherit eternal damnation, a judgment that only God can and will deliver.

Please remember that your soul is eternal, so try not to make decisions that will have a negative impact on your soul eternally. Surely, God has a very strong desire to establish and maintain a loving relationship with all of us. Who wouldn't? But God also loves you enough to let you make your own decisions and make up your own mind about who you will serve and where you will spend eternity. As long as you have breath in your body, you have the ability to get back on target. There is no sin too big for God to forgive if you ask Him for forgiveness from your heart. This is why Jesus came. He is our mediator, sitting between God's judgement and mankind, holding steady the hand of God over the earth. Those of us who believe in Jesus, we shall be saved; but to those who will not receive and obey Christ, in hell shall they lift up their eyes.

Do you really want to know if your soul is on track to hit the destination of heaven? What if I told you that you must first die to self? What if the requirement to even get on your mark and get set will cause you to lose somethings? In other words, reaching your goal will cause you to be sold out to Christ. Mathew 16:25 says, "For whosoever will save his life shall lose it: and whosoever will lose his life for my sake shall find it." If what you think and feel takes precedent over the Word of God but you still think you are going to heaven, then my friend you are sadly mistaken. God's Word is infallible and stands true with no help from man. It doesn't align itself with our thoughts and beliefs; we must align ourselves with its ways and precepts. When you attempt to manipulate God's Word to fit your desires, as the Scripture states, you will lose your life. This is actually a very dangerous position to be in because God will stand back and allow a person with such determination to walk right into their own trap and experience their own demise. Let's study for a moment a passage of warning to those who would try to redefine what God has deemed sinful and try to manipulate the Word of God to support man's opinions and beliefs. Romans 1:21-32 reads:

"...because that, when they knew God, they glorified Him not as God, neither were thankful; but became vain in their imaginations, and their foolish heart was darkened. Professing themselves to be wise, they became fools, and changed the glory of the incorruptible God into an image made like to corruptible man, and to birds, and four-footed beasts, and creeping things. Wherefore God also gave them up to uncleanness through the lusts of their own hearts, to dishonor their own bodies between themselves: who changed the truth of God into a lie, and worshipped and served the creature more than the Creator, who is blessed forever. Amen. For this cause God gave them up unto vile affections: For even their women did change the natural use into that which is against nature: And likewise also the men, leaving the natural use of the woman, burned in their lust one toward another; men with men working that which is unseemly, and receiving in themselves that recompense of their error which was meet. And even as they did not like to retain God in their knowledge, God gave them over to a reprobate mind, to do those things which are not convenient; Being filled with all unrighteousness, fornication, wickedness, covetousness, maliciousness; full of envy, murder, debate, deceit, malignity; whisperers, backbiters, haters of God, despiteful, proud, boasters, inventors of evil things, disobedient to parents, without understanding, covenant breakers, without natural affection, implacable, unmerciful: who knowing the judgment of God, that they which commit such things are worthy of death, not only do the same, but have pleasure in them that do them."

I have to be honest: this scripture details and outlines so many sins the world is now calling right and trying to endorse; and with the aid of a corrupt worldly system, many have found solace in their wrongdoing. Please take your time and read this passage so that you may gain a complete understanding. If you can't see God's urgent plea for misled sinners to repent due to His impending judgment upon sin then you simply don't Believe the Word of God. Bottom line is: Your life is lost due to your own disobedience to God's Word.

On the other hand, Jesus said, "If you lose your life for His name sake ye shall find it." Such encouraging words coming from our Savior who, one day, will separate those who are lost from those who have been found. Nothing is more comforting than knowing that our souls are in the hands of a loving God who will not let us be ashamed. In this text, the losing of one's life doesn't pertain to physical death, but rather, it refers to the giving up of one's selfish and sinful desires in order to be a servant of God. If we seek to please ourselves (flesh), then God receives no glory out of our lives; but if what pleases God becomes our main focus, then we glorify God in our lives. There is no life outside of Christ; for the Bible declares in Romans 6:23, "For the wages of sin is death; but the gift of God is eternal life through Jesus Christ our Lord."

In conclusion, I would like to admonish you to:

1. Get on target: Know the Word of God and do not compromise it for anything, not even your own thoughts. God's Word is sure, and He will stand by it and fulfill every promise and covenant therein.

2. Stay Focused: Life has so many distractions. But remember that it's not the distractions that causes us to fall, it's paying attention to them and taking our eyes off of Christ that causes us to sink.

3. Remember Christ: The purpose of Christ was to bring us back to the Father. He came to earth to feel and relate to what we go through as humans and to provide for us a clear example of how to conquer this world and its issues. But most importantly, Christ came to bring salvation to us and to help us develop a relationship with the Spirit of God. Lastly, Jesus Christ came to show us how to return home to the Father.

4. Live to Reach Eternity: Life is not just about the here and now. Remember: our decisions today will determine our eternal destinations. So choose ye this day who you will serve and where you will spend eternity.

WHAT IS YOUR SOUL'S TARGET?

CHAPTER THIRTEEN:
AM I ON TARGET FOR WHERE I WANT TO BE IN ETERNITY?
(WORK SECTION)

Now that we are at the end of the book, I need to ask you one very important question—and as Joshua stated in the Old Testament, you must "choose ye this day" what your answer is going to be: Where do you want to spend eternity?

Choose One: ☐ Heaven ☐ Hell
Peace & Comfort   Pain & Anguish

Have you been thinking about this question, and how much time do you feel you have to make a decision (if you haven't already done so)?

_____

_____

_____

_____

_____

_____

_____

_____

_____

_____

_____

_____

Some temporary decisions carry eternal consequences, but there are other decisions that may not send you to heaven or hell, but they could affect your effectiveness in carrying out God's will for your life. Name some of these temporary decisions:

_____

_____

_____

_____

_____

_____

When studying Romans 1:21-32, we see the dangers of turning our hearts from God and His Word (truth) in order to pursue our own wills. Explain what those verses are saying to you in detail:

_____

_____

_____

_____

_____

_____

_____

_____

_____

_____

_____

_____

_____

_____

_____

_____

_____

Final question: How has this book helped you and has it enlightened you in any way? Please send your response to:

mysoultarget@gmail.com

ABOUT THE AUTHOR

Styland Scott was born on August 6, 1975 in Savannah, Georgia to Henry and Elizabeth. At the age of two his family moved to Atlanta, Georgia where he was reared and completed grade school in the Atlanta Public School system. Being the son of a pastor, most of his time was spent in church, reading the Word of God, listening to sermons, and getting to know God on a personal level. After receiving a keyboard/piano for Christmas, he learned to play—he being self-taught. He would soon start playing for church services and developed a passion and love for music prompting him to practice hard and learn more. Styland began to play for school events, teach local community choirs, as well as direct district choirs and so much more. Upon graduation from North Atlanta School of Performing Arts, Styland joined the U.S. Armed Forces (Army) where he would start a new adventure in life. He completed his military career at Fort Stewart in Savannah, Georgia.

Never forgetting where he came from and his commitment and love for music and the arts, Styland continues to use his musical gifts, playing for chapel services in South Carolina,

Indiana, and all over Georgia, and even as far as South Korea. In 1998, Styland received the call from God into the ministry. He accepted it. Now ministering through song and the spoken Word of God, his life began to take shape with additional gifts and talents and his God-given purpose was revealed. In 2004, Styland wrote, produced, and directed his first stage play, "What God Allows", opening up a brand new avenue for him: gospel musicals. He has written and directed many stage plays since that time and continues to pursue the arts as a ministry for the Kingdom of God.

Several years after, while working in the ministry, he was ordained as a pastor in 2008 and started a church: Kingdom Advancement Ministries. While conducting a music workshop in Columbus, Georgia, he met his would-be wife, Valencia. After becoming the best of friends, falling in love, and understanding the purpose of their acquaintance, they joined in holy matrimony on February 25, 2012. This union would prove to be God's design as Styland would assume the office of Senior Pastor, Overseer, and Bishop of Kingdom Advancement Ministries and Day Star Temple Ministries. With his faithful wife by his side, Deuteronomy 32:30 took on a new meaning; "How should one chase a thousand, And two put ten thousand to flight, except their rock had given them over and the LORD had delivered them up?"

Serving faithfully in life's ministries, Styland is a dedicated employee of Fulton County Schools, a devoted husband, father, grandfather, musician, author, song writer, producer, and play write. He continues to focus on God and pleasing Him while helping to cultivate and push those around him to realize their full potential. Most of all, advancing the Kingdom of God through sound preaching, teaching, instructions, and doctrine is his life's mission. Styland continues to make disciples for Christ and strives to make a difference in the lives of those he meets daily.

CPSIA information can be obtained
at www.ICGtesting.com
Printed in the USA
FFOW01n1247240318
45903398-46786FF